The Sims
hot date
EXPANSION PACK

PRIMA'S OFFICIAL STRATEGY GUIDE

DAVID CHONG
MARK COHEN

Prima Games
A Division of Random House, Inc.

3000 Lava Ridge Court
Roseville, CA 95661
(916) 787-7000
www.primagames.com

Senior Product Manager: Jennifer Crotteau
Project Editor: Michelle Pritchard

ISBN: 0-7615-3729-5

Library of Congress Catalog Card Number: 2001096497

Printed in the United States of America

01 02 03 04 BB 10 9 8 7 6 5 4 3 2 1

Acknowledgments

This guide exists as a testament to the hard work and support put in by Jennifer Crotteau, Michelle Pritchard, David Mathews, and Asha Johnson. Special thanks to my friend and writing partner, Mark Cohen, who wrote the entire first part of the guide. The support I received from the Maxis team was stellar. I cannot overstate the value of the aid, insight, and support that Virginia McArthur, Sean Baity, Michael McCormick, Waylon Wilsonoff, and Roxy Wolosenko provided me. Finally, my deepest thanks go to my family for supporting my frenetic schedule on this project. My lovely Kate proves daily that best friends make the best spouses.

David Chong

Contents

INTRODUCTION: HOW TO USE THIS BOOK

Introduction

The Sims is not a game, it's a phenomenon. It has no end—none of the hundreds of thousands of people playing has ever "won" the game. With an unrivalled fan following and passionate support from its creators at Maxis, *The Sims* and its expansion packs have at times held all of the top spots in the computer game sales rankings. Clearly, the game has done something right.

This guide is not just a handbook for the *Hot Date* expansion pack, but a thorough companion for the entire game. There's a lot to consider in *The Sims* game world, and you'll want this guide by your side as long as you are playing the game. All of the game concepts are thoroughly explained to help you get started if you're new to *The Sims*, but we've also included in-depth resources that will serve as reference aids for even the most veteran Simmers. Much of the information on these tables is exclusive, never-before released insight into the inner workings of the game, including minimum relationship scores for interaction success, personality motivations, and more.

Part I: THE SIMS

This guide is split into two parts: *The Sims* (chapters 1–9) and *The Sims: Hot Date* (chapters 10–14). The first part introduces the original game and is a basic primer on all of the fundamental game concepts. Experienced players will still find many valuable reference tools in this part of the guide, clearly titled for easy reference.

Chapter 1, "What's Your Sim Sign?", explains how a Sim thinks, acts, and reacts in various situations. At the beginning of the game, you can mold your Sims' basic personalities, and we tell you how these traits affect their lives.

Chapter 2, "Motives—I Want, I Need; Therefore, I Am a Sim!", explains the eight primal urges that drive all Sims. We cover each one in detail, then blend the information with the previous chapter, so that you understand how a Sim's actions can be manipulated by you, and by other Sims.

Sims are very social creatures, and this can be a blessing or a curse. Chapter 3, "Interacting with Other Sims," shows you how and why a Sim interacts with others, and explains the benefits and pitfalls that accompany friendships, love relationships, and children.

Chapter 4, "9 to 5—Climbing the Career Ladder," looks at the working life of a Sim. You have myriad career choices and opportunities for advancement, and we provide you with the tools to get the job and promotions that will make your Sim financially successful.

Chapter 5, "Building a House," takes you through every step of the construction process, from putting up the framing to slapping on the final coat of paint. Our topics include walls, windows, doors, wall coverings, stairways and second stories, pools, and landscaping.

A Sim home is empty until you fill it with lots of stuff. Chapter 6, "Material Sims," provides facts and statistics on every object you can buy, more than 150 items in all. In addition to data and descriptions, we use detailed lists and tables to show how items relate to each other, and how some objects can even alter the effectiveness of other objects.

Now, it's time to put everything you know into action. We devote chapter 7, "All in the Family," and to describing the common and not-so-common events in a Sim's life. Get ready for a wild ride as we give you insights on single life, relationships, having children, and making friends.

Chapter 8, "A Day in the Life," follows a few of our families as they handle the ups and downs of Sim life. Check it out to see examples of our Sims in interesting situations.

Chapter 9, "Sim Survival Tips," is a quick-reference guide for times of crisis. Simply turn to the appropriate Motive and save your Sim's life with one of our game-tested tips. Or, if you're feeling devious, check out our cheats to satisfy your Sim's needs.

Part II: Hot Date

Hot Date is the quintessential expansion pack for *The Sims*, bringing the game into full realization of its incredible potential. The game has matured, and it plays a bit differently than the original game. It does this, however, without making you "unlearn" any of the original game features. This is accomplished through *growth* instead of outright *change*. Part II will help you get a handle on all the new game concepts, which affect all aspects of gameplay. Furthermore, you'll learn everything there is to know about dating, turning you into the hottest date in SimsVille!

Chapter 10, "Love is in the Air," provides you with a clear understanding of all the new facets of your Sims' personalities and relationships. *The Sims* is essentially a game about these two subjects, and *Hot Date* evolves them into full maturity. You'll learn about the new interaction trees, fully configurable interests, and all of the other details of the new social system. Better yet, you'll get exclusive info on all of the requirements for success for each interaction in the game!

Chapter 11, "Objects d'Amor," takes a look at the new objects included in *Hot Date*. Included is a buying guide to all of the new objects, plus strategies for using the new object types, including the prized ceiling-mounted lights.

You'll get the inside scoop on the features of the all-new downtown area in chapter 12, "City of Love." We've explored building strategies, planning considerations, and essential elements for shops, restaurants, and other attractions. You'll also find tips for incorporating the new building elements in your homes back in the neighborhoods.

Chapter 13, "City Slickers," introduces the NPCs that you'll meet in the *Hot Date* expansion pack. Dreamboats abound downtown, just waiting for the right Sim to sweep them off their feet. You'll also learn to spot the all-new service NPCs and get tips for interacting with them successfully.

Chapter 14, "A Night on the Town" covers every aspect of a *Hot Date*, from the moment your Sim wakes up in the pre-date morning to the final act. Will it be over with a drink in the face at the bar, or will your Sims make an even bigger splash in the Love Tub? You'll have the tools to decide for yourself with the dating strategies we reveal.

Finally, the guide culminates with chapter 15, "Extending Your World." Find suggestions for extending you Sim environment with special utilities and third party creations. You won't believe how many people are hooked on this game, and you'll be amazed at the thousands of new skins, heads, objects, homes, and wallpapers available to you…absolutely free on dozens of *Sims* websites.

In the appendix at the end of the guide, we've also included a golden key: the Interaction Menu Triggers table. This exclusive info is so good it's almost naughty, so we've moved it out of the main text. This way, you can decide whether or not you want to sneak a peek! With this table, you'll know exactly how to get any interaction in the game to come up as an option in your social pie menus. With the mystery of the interaction triggers unlocked, you'll be dip kissing and slapfighting in no time!

PART 1:

CHAPTER 1:
WHAT'S YOUR SIM SIGN?

Introduction

When you are charged with the solemn task of creating a Sim from scratch, you have 25 points to distribute over five traits: Neat, Outgoing, Active, Playful, and Nice. Whether we admit it or not, all of us have an inherent wish to be perfectly balanced people (or Sims). Of course, you can take the easy way out and award five points in every category, creating a generic Sim. You'll spend less time managing a middle-of-the-road Sim because in most situations, he or she will do the right thing. If you'd rather play it safe, skip this chapter and move right to "Motives: I Want...I Need...Therefore, I Am a Sim". If not, read on as we describe the subtle (and sometimes dramatic) outcomes that your personality ratings will inspire.

It's in the Stars

As you play with the personality bars, you'll note the changing zodiac sign that appears on the screen. Of course, a serious astrologer would argue that a true personality profile is based on much more than five traits. However, if you have a basic understanding of newspaper horoscopes, you'll be able to recognize yourself, or someone close to you, as you create a Sim personality. In the next section we'll look at each trait and examine the potential effects of your ratings in various game situations. But first, let's take a look at basic interpersonal compatibility as seen through the eyes of the zodiac. The following table gives you the best and worst matchups for friends and lovers. This doesn't necessarily imply that any other Relationship outside of the table is doomed; it is merely an indication of how hard you'll have to work on it.

Sims Zodiac Compatibility Table

SIGN	ATTRACTED TO	REPELLED BY
Aries	Gemini/Taurus	Cancer/Libra
Taurus	Aries/Libra	Virgo/Cancer
Gemini	Pisces/Virgo	Capricorn/Aries
Cancer	Taurus/Scorpio	Gemini/Aries
Virgo	Aquarius/Sagittarius	Leo/Taurus
Libra	Virgo/Cancer	Pisces/Scorpio
Scorpio	Pisces/Leo	Libra/Aquarius
Sagittarius	Pisces/Capricorn	Libra/Scorpio
Leo	Sagittarius/Cancer	Capricorn/Gemini
Capricorn	Aquarius/Taurus	Leo/Gemini
Aquarius	Capricorn/Sagittarius	Scorpio/Virgo
Pisces	Scorpio/Gemini	Leo/Aries

Personality Traits

The following sections review what you can expect from each type of Sim, with examples of how different personality traits will manifest during the game. For our purposes, we'll divide the ratings bar into three sections: Low (1–3), Average (4–7), and High (8–10). These numbers correspond to the number of light blue bars to the right of each trait.

Neat

Low

Don't expect these Sims to pick up their dirty dishes, wash their hands after using the bathroom, or take timely showers. They are perfectly content to let others clean up their messes.

Fig. 1-1. The kitchen floor is a perfect place for this messy Sim's snack leavings.

Fig. 1-3. This fastidious Sim goes straight to the bathtub after a hard day's work.

Medium

At least these Sims keep themselves relatively clean, and you can depend on them to clean up their own messes. Occasionally they'll even clean up another Sim's garbage, but you might have to intervene if you have several cleanup items that need attention.

Outgoing

Low

Shy, reserved, Sims have less pressing needs for Social interaction, so it will be more difficult to pursue friendships with other Sims, although they can still carry on stimulating conversations. Within their own home, a shy Sim may be less interested in receiving hugs, kisses, and back rubs, so if you are looking for romance, it would be a good idea to find a compatible target (see zodiac chart on p. 2).

Fig. 1-2. After slopping water all over the bathroom during his shower, this moderately neat Sim mops up his mess before leaving the room.

Fig. 1-4. This Sim cringes at the thought of a back rub—poor guy.

High

A super-neat Sim always checks the vicinity for dirty dishes and old newspapers, and of course, personal hygiene is a big priority. One of these Sims can compensate for one or two slobs in a household.

Medium

It will be a little easier to get this Sim to mix with strangers and enjoy a little intimacy from his housemates. Don't expect a party animal, but you'll be able to entice your guests into most activities.

Fig. 1-5. Come on everyone, let's hit the pool!

High

This Sim needs plenty of Social stimulation to prevent his or her Social score from plummeting. You'll have no trouble throwing parties or breaking the ice with just about any personality type.

.

Fig. 1-6. This outgoing Sim is still unconscious from last night's pool party, and she has inspired the close friendship of another man. Hmmm.

Active

Low

Forget about pumping iron or swimming 100 laps at 5:00 a.m. These Sims prefer a soft easy chair to a hard workout. A sofa and a good TV are high on their priority list. In fact, if they don't get their daily ration of vegging, their Comfort scores will suffer.

Fig. 1-7. This Sim says "No way!" to a session on the exercise bench.

Medium

These Sims strike a good balance between relaxing and breaking a sweat. They dance, swim, and even shoot hoops without expressing discomfort.

Fig. 1-8. His Active rating is only a four, but that doesn't stop this Sim from shooting hoops in his jammies.

High

Active Sims like to pick up the pace rather than fall asleep on the sofa in front of the TV. Get these Sims a pool, basketball hoop, or exercise bench, and plan on dancing the night away with friends.

Fig. 1-9. Even in her business suit, this active Sim will gladly leave Mortimer on the sofa and pump some iron in the backyard.

Medium

These well-rounded Sims are usually receptive to a good joke and don't mind a little tickling. They may not be the first ones on the dance floor, but they'll join in with a good crowd.

Fig. 1-11. This Sim is Playful enough to dance, even though she is overdue for a shower.

Playful

Low

Get these Sims a bookcase, a comfortable chair, and plenty of books. If reading isn't an option, looking at a painting or playing a game of chess will do just fine.

Fig. 1-10. There's always time to watch the fish, for this less-than-playful Sim.

High

Can you spell P-A-R-T-Y? These Sims love to have a few drinks, dance to good music, and invite lots of guests over to the house. They love telling jokes, and they are usually ready to laugh at others' stories.

Fig. 1-12. This Playful kid would get the Maid in the pool for a game of chicken, if only she would respond.

Nice

Low

There is nothing redeeming about a grouchy Sim. They are always ready to tease or insult their friends, and they love to brag. A Sim with a low Nice rating should be dropped from your guest list immediately, or asked to leave if he or she shows up.

Fig. 1-13. Usually a compliment elicits a nice response, but not so with with sourpuss.

Medium

This Sim keeps an even keel about most things. Of all the traits, Nice is the least destructive if you award at least four points. Only the nastiest Sims can get under a medium-Nice Sim's skin.

Fig. 1-14. This Sim has time for a good tickle, even while mopping up the bathroom.

High

These Sims just want to make the world a better place for everyone. If there was a Sim beauty contest, the winner would be extremely "Nice."

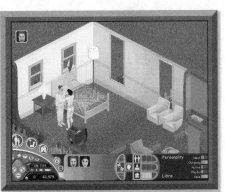

Fig. 1-15. Even after spending the night on the kitchen floor, this Sim still knows how to compliment her mate.

Personality Tables

The following tables demonstrate how personality traits affect Fun scores and Skill development.

Traits that Raise Max Fun Value

PERSONALITY TRAIT	RAISES MAX FUN SCORE FOR
Playful	Aquarium, Chess Table, Computer, Doll House, Flamingo, Pinball, TV (Cartoon Channel), VR Glasses
Serious (Low Playful)	Newspaper (Read)
Active	Basketball Hoop, Play Structure, TV (Action Channel)
Outgoing	Hot Tub, TV (Romance Channel)
Grouchy (Low Nice)	TV (Horror Channel)

Skills Accelerated by Personality

SKILL	OBJECTS USED TO INCREASE SKILL	TRAIT ACCELERATOR
Creativity	Easel, Piano	Playful
Body	Exercise Machine, Swimming Pool	Active
Charisma	Medicine Cabinet, Mirrors	Outgoing

CHAPTER 2: MOTIVES—I WANT, I NEED; THEREFORE, I AM A SIM!

Introduction

When you consider how many needs, traits, and desires make up a Sim's personality, it would be an injustice to call it AI. Never before has a computer-generated character interacted so completely with both the game and the gamer while maintaining a unique (and ever-changing) personality. Is it any wonder that *The Sims* has topped the PC sales chart for nearly two years running?

In the previous chapter we discussed a Sim's personality traits. It painted a broad picture of the various types of Sims you might encounter in the game, much the same as a newspaper horoscope tells a superficial story of a person's life. In this chapter, we advance from broad-brush personality traits to the eight powerful Motives that drive a Sim's every action. We cover each Motive in detail, but first, let's begin with a few basic definitions.

What Is a Motive?

A Motive is, very simply, a need. Your Sims follow these needs, based on their own instincts and a little help from you. If you activate Free Will in the Options menu, your Sims will also make their own decisions, based on changing needs. After selecting a Motive to fulfill, be it Hunger or Hygiene, the Sim is "rewarded" with Motive points. These points raise the corresponding Motive score.

The eight Motive scores are displayed on the right side of the control panel. A Motive rating is considered positive if the bar is green, and negative if it is red. Internally, the game uses a 200-point system, with positive (green) ratings between 0 and 100, and negative (red) ratings from 0 to -100.

> ## TIP
> When any of the Sims' eight Motives drop below a certain level, a Sim will cease an activity that doesn't improve the Motive in distress. So, you'll see low-priority items drop out of the activity queue, or your Sim will add an activity that addresses the critical need.

> ## CAUTION
> *Without Free Will, your Sims depend entirely on your input to keep them alive. If you don't tell them to eat, they will starve, and eventually die.*

Mood Rating

The game control panel also displays a Mood Rating, just to the right of the Sim character icons. If the rating is positive, you see up to five green bars displayed above the comedy/tragedy masks. When the Mood Rating is negative, it displays up to five red bars below the masks.

In calculating the Mood Rating, each of the eight Motives is weighted, based on how critical it is to sustaining a Sim's life. Hence, Hunger, Bladder, and Energy, which are all related to a Sim's physical well-being, carry more weight than the noncritical Motives such as Social, Fun, or Room. So, if a Sim is hungry and tired, as pictured in figure 2-1, the overall Mood Rating will be relatively low, even if several other Motives are high.

Fig. 2-1. This Sim kid's overall Mood Rating is barely positive, due to the fact that he is starving and low on Energy.

The Motives

In the following sections we describe the eight Motives, using several tables to show you how and why a Sim reacts to different objects in the environment. By recognizing the relationships between Motives and objects, you'll begin to understand how a Sim considers a perpetual barrage of options. Once you do this, the only remaining question is, "Who is really in charge here, you or the Sim?"

Fig. 2-2. This Sim family enjoys a meal together. Mom's Hunger bar is in the worst shape, so she has a second meal plate at the ready.

NOTE

Aside from the overall Motive weighting system, each Sim suffers different rates of Motive depreciation based on personality traits. For example, a Playful Sim must have more "rewards" to maintain the Fun Motive bar. Similarly, an Outgoing Sim requires more interaction with other Sims to maintain the Social score.

Hunger Score for Each Meal, Snack, or Gift

MEAL TYPE	HUNGER MOTIVE BAR POINTS
Snack	9
Quick Meal	16
Full Meal	16
Group Meal (per serving)	16
Pizza (per serving)	33
Candy Box (gift)	3 (per serving, 12 servings per box)
Fruitcake (gift)	7 (per slice, 6 slices per box)

Hunger

For obvious reasons, a Sim cannot survive for very long without food. We'll cover the details of food preparation in a later chapter, but for now let's focus on the basics. As long as you have a refrigerator, a Sim can enjoy a Snack, Quick Meal, Full Meal, or Group Meal (same as a Full Meal, except one of the Sims prepares several servings). In addition to preparing food, a Sim with a telephone can order out for Pizza, or enjoy food that was brought as a gift (Candy Box or Fruitcake). The Hunger Motive bar points awarded with each meal are outlined in the following table.

Comfort

The next category listed in the Needs section of the control panel is considerably less important than Hunger. Sims like to be comfortable, and they love cushy chairs, oversized sofas, and supportive beds. Spending more money on these objects translates into greater Motive rewards. However, if your budget is tight, you must still furnish the house with basic furniture or your Sims will express their discomfort.

Fig. 2-3. With only a cheap chair and loveseat, this Sim's Comfort score is mired in the red.

Fig. 2-4. Three out of four Motive scores are on the way up while this couple enjoys a hot tub soak.

Hunger, Bladder, Energy, and Comfort are the most demanding of Motives, because if any one score drops below a certain level, the Sim will immediately exit his or her current activity to remedy the deficit. The following table lists the exit triggers for each category.

Mandatory Exit Factors

MOTIVE	SIM TYPE	EXITS CURRENT INTERACTION WHEN MOTIVE DROPS BELOW
Bladder	Resident	-85
Bladder	Visitor	-80
Comfort	Resident	-90
Comfort	Visitor	-60
Energy	Resident	-80
Energy	Visitor	-70
Hunger	Resident	-80
Hunger	Visitor	-40

Hygiene

Bad Hygiene will never kill a Sim, although it may seriously gross out others in the immediate vicinity. Solving this problem is easy—have your Sims wash their hands or take a shower. You can also combine Hygiene with other Motives. Taking a bath boosts the Hygiene and Comfort scores, while a soak in the hot tub (with friends) rewards the Hygiene, Comfort, Social, and Fun Motive bars.

Bladder

If you can't satisfy the Bladder urge, you'll be cleaning up puddles on the floor. Just make sure you find a bathroom before the Motive bar turns full red. A Sloppy Sim creates an additional risk by not regularly flushing the toilet. If you don't issue timely reminders, the toilet could get clogged, causing a major mess.

TIP

Pay special attention to the Bladder bar when your Sim spends time at the Beverage Bar or drinks a lot of coffee.

CAUTION

The Hygiene score takes a nose dive if a Sim can't get to the bathroom in time and pees on the floor.

Fig. 2-5. This Sim's Bladder is not quite full, but unless his guest vacates the bathroom soon, he could be in trouble.

Energy

We're talking sleep, pure and simple. Ideally, a good night's sleep should turn the bar completely green. This will happen at varying rates, depending upon the quality of the mattress, so you can get by on less sleep if you splurge for an expensive bed. If your Sim can't get to the bedroom or a couch before the Energy bar turns completely red, the floor becomes your only option. If this happens, wake your Sim and find the closest bed. A night on the hard floor will degrade your Sim's Comfort level to zero, while only restoring partial energy.

If your Sim stays up too late playing computer games, a shot of espresso provides a temporary Energy boost, although it will also fill the Bladder at an increased rate. Espresso has a powerful effect, but it takes longer to consume, which could be a problem if the car pool driver is honking.

Fig. 2-6. It never hurts to send your kids to bed early, because if they are tired in the morning, a coffee jolt is not an option.

Fun

Sims like to cut loose from the daily grind and have Fun, but depending upon their personalities, they prefer different activities. For example, a Playful Sim leans toward computer games, pinball machines, and train sets; while a more Serious Sim would rather sit down to a quiet game of chess or spend a few minutes gazing at a painting.

Fig. 2-7. These two Sims enjoy a game of pool after work.

Kids need to have more Fun than adults, and the effects of a single play session deteriorate faster for kids than for their older counterparts. Hence, it is a good idea to fill the house with plenty of juvenile diversions if you have children.

There are four different types of Fun activities: Extended, One-Time, Timed, and Endless. The following lists and tables provide additional information, including exit factors, for these pursuits.

Extended Fun Activities

Sims exit the following extended activities after reaching the maximum Fun score for their personality types. Hence, a Playful, Active Sim will stay on the basketball court longer than a Serious Sim.

- Basketball Hoop
- Bookshelf (reading)
- Dollhouse
- Computer (playing games)
- Pinball Machine
- Play Structure
- Stereo
- Toy Box
- Train Set
- TV
- VR Glasses

One-Time Fun Activities

The following activities raise a Sim's Fun score once with each interaction. It may take several interactions with the same activity for a Sim to reach the maximum Fun level.

OBJECT	ACTION
Aquarium	Feed or watch fish
Baby	Play
Diving Board	Dive into the pool
Espresso Machine	Drink espresso
Fountain	View
Lava Lamp	View
Painting	View
Sculpture	View

Timed (Pre-set) Fun Activities

As with the one-time activities listed above, a Sim may need to repeat the following activities to achieve maximum Fun points.

- Chess Set
- Pool Table

Endless Fun

- **Hot Tub:** A Sim will stay in the tub until Fun, Comfort, Social, and Hygiene numbers reach maximum levels.
- **Swimming Pool:** A Sim will keep doing laps until another Motive takes effect, or until you assign him or her to another activity.

Social

Sims crave other Sims, especially if they are Outgoing. Although they won't die without socializing, it is a good idea to devote a portion of each day to a group activity, even if it is a simple hot tub session with your Sim's mate, or a family meal.

Fig. 2-8. A casual conversation during breakfast raises this Sim's Social score.

The following table summarizes all of the possible Social interactions between adults and children. We take this one step further in the next chapter, "Interacting with Other Sims," where we examine Relationships.

Adult-Child Interactions

ACTION	ADULT TO ADULT	CHILD TO CHILD	ADULT TO CHILD	CHILD TO ADULT
Apologize	X	—	—	—
Attack	X	X	—	—
Brag	X	X	X	X
Call Here	X	X	X	X
Cheer Up	X	X	X	X
Compliment	X	—	—	—
Dance	X	—	—	—
Entertain	X	X	X	X
Flirt	X	—	—	—
Give Back Rub	X	—	—	—
Give Gift	X	X	X	X
Hug	X	X	X	X
Insult	X	X	X	X
Joke	X	X	X	X
Kiss	X	—	—	—
Say Goodbye	X	X	X	—
Scare	X	X	X	X
Slap	X	—	—	—
Tag	—	X	—	—
Talk	X	X	X	X
Tease	X	X	X	X
Tickle	X	X	X	X

Social Outcome Modifiers

You didn't expect a Sim Social encounter to be simple, did you? When one Sim communicates with another, several calculations determine the outcome. Factors include age (adult or child), sex, mood, and personality traits, not to mention the current state of their Relationship. Also, a Sim with strong Social needs (but few friends) may expect more from an encounter with a Sim who has similar needs.

The following table lists the factors that govern the choices that appear on a Social actions menu. For example, two Sims who are strangers are not likely to have the options to kiss or hug. Additionally, the table lists key factors that determine the eventual outcome.

rel = Relationship

out = Outgoing

play = Playful

ff = Friend Flag

ss = Same Sex

rom = Romance Flag

age = Adult/Child

social = Social Motive Value

vis = Visitor

budget = Household Budget

nice = Nice

body = Body

Social Outcome Factors

INTERACTION	FACTORS THAT DETERMINE APPEARANCE ON THE MENU	FACTORS THAT DETERMINE OUTCOME
Apologize	rel	mood
Attack	age, nice, mood, rel	body
Back Rub	age, nice, mood, rel, out, ss	rel, out, ss
Brag	nice, out, social, rel	rel, mood
Cheer Up	ff, mood (of friend), nice	rel
Compliment	age, nice, out, mood, rel	rel, mood
Dance	age, mood, out, rel	rel, out, mood
Entertain	social, out, play, mood, rel	play, rel
Flirt	age, social, ss, out, mood, rel, rom	rel, mood, ss
Gift	vis, budget, nice, mood, rel	rel, mood
Hug	age, out, mood, rel, ss	rel, out, mood, ss
Insult	nice, mood, rel	nice
Joke	play, mood, rel	play, mood, rel
Kiss	ss, mood, rel, age	rel, mood, ss
Scare	nice, mood, play, rel	play, mood
Slap	age, nice, mood, rel	nice, mood
Talk	mood, rel, out	topics match
Tease	nice, mood, rel	rel, mood
Tickle	social, out, play, active, mood, rel	rel, play

Room

This is a combined rating that analyzes the design and contents of the current room, and translates it into a Room score. Of all the Motives, Room is the least important. However, if you love your Sim, you'll want to create the best possible environment. The most important contributing factors to Room score are:

- **Light:** Sims hate dark rooms, so fill your house with sunlight (windows and paned doors), lamps, and wall lights.
- **Room Size:** Don't cramp your Sims into tiny rooms.
- **Corners:** As mentioned in the "Building a House" chapter, Sims love corners.
- **State of Repair:** Any items that are not functioning properly detract from the Room score (see following list).

Fig. 2-9. Who wouldn't love a kitchen like this? It's bright, roomy, nicely furnished, and packed with high-tech appliances.

Negative Impact on Room Score

- **Trash**
- **Floods**
- **Dirty plates**
- **Meals with flies**
- **Full trash cans/compactors**
- **Dead plants**
- **Puddle or ash pile**
- **Dead fish in aquariums**
- **Dirty objects (shower, toilet, tub)**

The following table lists the positive or negative value of every object in *The Sims*.

Room Score

OBJECT	STATE/TYPE	ROOM SCORE
Aquarium	Fish Alive	25
	Dirty	-25
	Dirty and/or Dead	-50
Ash	N/A	-10
Bar	N/A	20
Bed	Unmade (Any Bed)	-10
	Made Mission	30
	Made (Other than Mission)	10
Chair	Parisienne	25
	Empress	10
Clock (Grandfather)	N/A	50
Computer	Broken	-25
Counter	Barcelona	15
Desk	Redmond	15
Dresser	Antique Armoire	20
	Oak Armoire	10
Fire	N/A	-100

OBJECT	STATE/TYPE	ROOM SCORE
Fireplace	Library Edition (No Fire)	20
	Library Edition (Fire)	75
	Worcestershire (No Fire)	15
	Worcestershire (Fire)	60
	Bostonian (No Fire)	10
	Bostonian (Fire)	45
	Modesto (No Fire)	5
	Modesto (Fire)	30
Flamingo	N/A	10
Flood	N/A	-25
Flowers (Outdoor)	Healthy	20
	Dead	-20
Flowers/Plants (Indoor)	Healthy	10
	Wilted	0
	Dead	-10
Food	Snack (Spoiled)	-15
	Fruitcake (Empty Plate)	-5
	BBQ Group Meal (Spoiled)	-20
	BBQ Single Meal (Spoiled)	-15
	Empty Plate	-10
	Pizza Slice (Spoiled)	-10
	Pizza Box (Spoiled)	-25
	Candy (Spoiled)	-5
	Group Meal (Spoiled)	-20
	Meal (Spoiled)	-25
	Quick Meal (Spoiled)	-20
Fountain	N/A	25
Flowers (Gift)	Dead	-10
	Alive	20
Lamp	Not Broken	10
Lava Lamp	N/A	20
Newspaper	Old Newspapers	-20
Piano	N/A	30

OBJECT	STATE/TYPE	ROOM SCORE
Pinball Machine	Broken	-15
Shower	Broken	-15
Sofa (Deiter or Dolce)	N/A	20
Stereo	Strings	25
Table	Mesa	15
	Parisienne	25
Toilet	Clogged	-10
Train Set	Small	25
Trash Can (Inside)	Full	-20
Trash Compactor	Full	-25
Trash Pile	N/A	-20
TV	Soma	20
	Broken (Any TV)	-15

Object Advertising Values

Earlier in the chapter we mentioned that Sims receive Motive rewards when they select an activity. If you are in complete control of your Sims (Free Will is off), you determine their choices. However, with Free Will on, Sims constantly poll their surroundings to compare which objects are "advertising" the most attractive rewards. The following table includes a Motive profile of every object in *The Sims*.

Object Advertising Values

OBJECT TYPE	POSSIBLE INTERACTIONS	OBJECT VARIATIONS	ADVERTISED MOTIVE	ADVERTISED VALUE	PERSONALITY TRAIT MODIFIER	REDUCED EFFECTS (OVER DISTANCE)
Aquarium	Clean & Restock	N/A	Room	30	Neat	Medium
	Feed Fish	N/A	Room	10	Nice	High
		N/A	Fun	10	Playful	High
	Watch Fish	N/A	Fun	10	Playful	High
Ash	Sweep Up	N/A	Energy	23	N/A	Medium
		N/A	Room	50	Neat	Medium
Baby	Play	N/A	Fun	50	Playful	Medium
Bar	Have Drink	N/A	Room	30	N/A	Low
	Grill	Barbecue	Energy	-10	N/A	Low
			Hunger	40	Cooking	Low
Basketball Hoop	Join	N/A	Fun	30	Active	High
		N/A	Social	20	N/A	Medium
		N/A	Energy	-20	N/A	Medium
	Play	N/A	Fun	30	Active	High
		N/A	Energy	-20	N/A	High
Bed	Make Bed	All Beds	Room	25	Neat	High
	Sleep	Double Bed (Cheap Eazzzzze)	Energy	65	N/A	None
		Double Bed (Napoleon)	Energy	67	N/A	None
		Double Bed (Mission)	Energy	70	N/A	None
		Single Bed (Spartan)	Energy	60	N/A	None
		Single Bed (Tyke Nyte)	Energy	63	N/A	None
	Tuck in Kid	All Beds	Energy	160	Nice	None

OBJECT TYPE	POSSIBLE INTERACTIONS	OBJECT VARIATIONS	ADVERTISED MOTIVE	ADVERTISED VALUE	PERSONALITY TRAIT MODIFIER	REDUCED EFFECTS (OVER DISTANCE)
Bookcase	Read a Book	Bookcase (Pine)	Fun	10	Serious	High
		Bookcase (Amishim)	Fun	20	Serious	High
		Bookcase (Libri di Regina)	Fun	30	Serious	High
Chair (Living Room)	Sit	Wicker	Comfort	20	N/A	Medium
		Country Class	Comfort	20	N/A	Medium
		Citronel	Comfort	20	N/A	Medium
		Sarrbach	Comfort	20	N/A	Medium
Chair (Dining Room)	Sit	Werkbunnst	Comfort	25	N/A	Medium
		Teak	Comfort	25	N/A	Medium
		Empress	Comfort	25	N/A	Medium
		Parisienne	Comfort	25	N/A	Medium
Chair (Office/Deck)	Sit	Office Chair	Comfort	20	N/A	Medium
		Deck Chair	Comfort	20	N/A	Medium
Chair (Recliner)	Nap	Both Recliners	Energy	15	Lazy	High
		Both Recliners	Comfort	20	Lazy	Medium
	Sit	Both Recliners	Comfort	30	Lazy	Medium
Chess	Join	Chess Set	Fun	40	Outgoing	High
			Social	40	N/A	Medium
	Play		Fun	35	Serious	High
Clock (Grandfather)	Wind	N/A	Room	40	Neat	High
Coffee (Espresso Machine)	Drink Espresso	N/A	Energy	115	N/A	Medium
		N/A	Fun	10	N/A	High
		N/A	Bladder	-10	N/A	High
Coffeemaker	Drink Coffee	N/A	Bladder	-5	N/A	High
		N/A	Energy	115	N/A	Medium

OBJECT TYPE	POSSIBLE INTERACTIONS	OBJECT VARIATIONS	ADVERTISED MOTIVE	ADVERTISED VALUE	PERSONALITY TRAIT MODIFIER	REDUCED EFFECTS (OVER DISTANCE)
Computer	Play	Moneywell	Fun	30	Playful	High
		Microscotch	Fun	35	Playful	High
		Brahma	Fun	40	Playful	High
		Marco	Fun	50	Playful	High
	Turn Off	All Computers	Energy	220	Neat	Medium
Dollhouse	Play	N/A	Fun	30	Playful	High
	Watch	N/A	Fun	30	Playful	Medium
		N/A	Social	30	N/A	Medium
Easel	Paint	N/A	Fun	20	N/A	High
Flamingo	Kick	N/A	Mood	15	Grouchy	High
	View	N/A	Fun	10	Playful	High
Flood	Clean	N/A	Room	80	Neat	High
Flowers (Outdoor)	Stomp On	N/A	Mood	10	Grouchy	High
	Water	N/A	Room	20	Neat	Medium
Flowers/Plants (Indoor)	Throw Out	N/A	Room	50	Neat	Medium
	Water	N/A	Room	25	Neat	Medium
Food	Clean	All Meal/ Snack Types	Room	20	Neat	Medium
	Prepare and Eat	BBQ Group Meal	Hunger	90	N/A	Low
		BBQ Single	Hunger	80	N/A	Low
		Candy	Hunger	30	N/A	Low
		Fruitcake (Group Meal)	Hunger	30	N/A	Low
		Fruitcake (Slice)	Hunger	80	N/A	Low
		Light Meal	Hunger	80	N/A	Low
		Pizza Box	Hunger	90	N/A	Low
		Pizza Slice	Hunger	80	N/A	Low
		Regular Group Meal	Hunger	90	N/A	Low
		Regular Single Meal	Hunger	80	N/A	Low
		Snack	Hunger	25	N/A	Low

OBJECT TYPE	POSSIBLE INTERACTIONS	OBJECT VARIATIONS	ADVERTISED MOTIVE	ADVERTISED VALUE	PERSONALITY TRAIT MODIFIER	REDUCED EFFECTS (OVER DISTANCE)
Fountain	Play	N/A	Fun	10	Shy	High
Refrigerator	Have Meal	All Fridges	Hunger	65	N/A	Low
	Have Snack	Llamark	Hunger	20	N/A	Low
		Porcina	Hunger	30	N/A	Low
		Freeze Secret	Hunger	40	N/A	Low
	Have Quick Meal	All Fridges	Hunger	55	N/A	Low
	Serve Meal	All Fridges	Hunger	70	Cooking	Low
		All Fridges	Energy	-10	N/A	Low
Gift (Flowers)	Clean	N/A	Room	30	Neat	Medium
Hot Tub	Get In	N/A	Fun	45	Lazy	High
		N/A	Comfort	50	N/A	High
		N/A	Social	25	Outgoing	Medium
		N/A	Hygiene	5	N/A	Medium
	Join	N/A	Comfort	30	N/A	Low
		N/A	Fun	50	Outgoing	Low
		N/A	Social	50	N/A	Low
		N/A	Hygiene	5	N/A	Medium
Lava Lamp	Turn On	N/A	Room	5	N/A	High
		N/A	Fun	5	N/A	High
Mailbox	Get Mail	N/A	Comfort	10	N/A	High
		N/A	Hunger	10	N/A	High
		N/A	Hygiene	10	N/A	High
		N/A	Room	10	N/A	High
Medicine Cabinet	Brush Teeth	N/A	Hygiene	25	Neat	Medium
Newspaper	Clean Up	N/A	Room	50	Neat	Medium
	Read	N/A	Fun	5	Serious	High
Painting	View	N/A	Fun	5	Serious	High
Phone	Answer	N/A	Fun	50	N/A	Medium
		N/A	Comfort	50	N/A	Medium
		N/A	Social	50	N/A	Medium
Piano	Play	N/A	Fun	40	Strong Creativity	High
	Watch	N/A	Fun	70	N/A	Medium
		N/A	Social	10	N/A	Medium

OBJECT TYPE	POSSIBLE INTERACTIONS	OBJECT VARIATIONS	ADVERTISED MOTIVE	ADVERTISED VALUE	PERSONALITY TRAIT MODIFIER	REDUCED EFFECTS (OVER DISTANCE)
Pinball Machine	Join	N/A	Fun	50	N/A	Medium
		N/A	Social	30	N/A	Medium
	Play	N/A	Fun	40	Playful	High
Play Structure	Join	N/A	Fun	60	Playful	Medium
		N/A	Social	40	N/A	Medium
	Play	N/A	Fun	60	Playful	Medium
Pool Diving Board	Dive In	N/A	Fun	35	Active	High
		N/A	Energy	-10	N/A	High
Pool Table	Join	N/A	Fun	50	Playful	Low
		N/A	Social	40	N/A	Low
	Play	N/A	Fun	45	Playful	High
Sculpture	View	Scylla and Charybdis	Fun	6	Serious	High
		Bust of Athena	Fun	5	Serious	High
		Large Black Slab	Fun	8	Serious	High
		China Vase	Fun	7	Serious	High
Shower	Clean	N/A	Room	20	Neat	High
	Take a Shower	N/A	Hygiene	50	Neat	Medium
Sink	Wash Hands	N/A	Hygiene	10	Neat	High
Sofa/Loveseat	Nap	All Sofas/ Loveseats	Energy	40	Lazy	High
		All Sofas/ Loveseats	Comfort	5	Lazy	High
	Sit	All Sofas/ Loveseats	Comfort	30	Lazy	Medium
		Garden Bench	Comfort	30	Lazy	Medium
Stereo	Dance	Boom Box	Social	40	Outgoing	High
			Fun	50	Active	High
		Zimantz Hi-Fi	Social	50	Outgoing	High
			Fun	60	Active	High
		Strings Theory	Social	60	Outgoing	High
			Fun	70	Active	High
	Join	Boom Box	Social	40	Outgoing	Low

OBJECT TYPE	POSSIBLE INTERACTIONS	OBJECT VARIATIONS	ADVERTISED MOTIVE	ADVERTISED VALUE	PERSONALITY TRAIT MODIFIER	REDUCED EFFECTS (OVER DISTANCE)
Stereo			Fun	40	Outgoing	Low
		Zimantz Hi-Fi	Social	50	Outgoing	Low
			Fun	40	Outgoing	Low
		Strings Theory	Social	60	Outgoing	Low
			Fun	40	Outgoing	Low
	Turn Off	All Stereos	Energy	220	Neat	Medium
	Turn On	Boom Box	Fun	25	Playful	High
		Zimantz Hi-Fi	Fun	25	Playful	High
		Strings Theory	Fun	30	Playful	High
Toilet	Clean	Both Toilets	Room	40	Neat	High
	Flush	Hygeia-O-Matic	Room	30	Neat	High
	Unclog	Both Toilets	Room	50	Neat	High
	Use	Hygeia-O-Matic	Bladder	50	N/A	Low
		Flush Force	Bladder	70	N/A	Low
Tombstone/ Urn	Mourn (first 24 hours)	N/A	Bladder	5	N/A	Low
		N/A	Comfort	50	N/A	Low
		N/A	Energy	5	N/A	Low
		N/A	Fun	50	N/A	Low
		N/A	Hunger	5	N/A	Low
		N/A	Hygiene	50	N/A	Low
		N/A	Social	50	N/A	Low
		N/A	Room	50	N/A	Low
	Mourn (second 48 hours)	N/A	Bladder	0	N/A	Low
		N/A	Comfort	30	N/A	Low
		N/A	Energy	0	N/A	Low
		N/A	Fun	30	N/A	Low
		N/A	Hunger	0	N/A	Low
		N/A	Hygiene	30	N/A	Low
		N/A	Social	30	N/A	Low
		N/A	Room	30	N/A	Low
Toy Box	Play	N/A	Fun	55	Playful	Medium

OBJECT TYPE	POSSIBLE INTERACTIONS	OBJECT VARIATIONS	ADVERTISED MOTIVE	ADVERTISED VALUE	PERSONALITY TRAIT MODIFIER	REDUCED EFFECTS (OVER DISTANCE)
Train Set (Large)	Play	N/A	Fun	40	N/A	Medium
	Watch	N/A	Fun	40	N/A	Low
		N/A	Social	40	N/A	Low
Train Set (Small)	Play	N/A	Fun	45	Playful	Medium
	Watch	N/A	Fun	20	N/A	Medium
		N/A	Social	30	N/A	Medium
Trash Can (Inside)	Empty Trash	N/A	Room	30	Neat	Medium
Trash Compactor	Empty Trash	N/A	Room	30	N/A	High
Trash Pile	Clean	N/A	Room	75	Neat	Medium
Bathtub	Clean	All Tubs	Room	20	Neat	High
	Bathe	Justa	Hygiene	50	Neat	Medium
		Justa	Comfort	20	N/A	Medium
		Sani-Queen	Hygiene	60	Neat	Medium
		Sani-Queen	Comfort	25	N/A	Medium
		Hydrothera	Hygiene	70	Neat	Medium
		Hydrothera	Comfort	30	N/A	Medium
TV	Join	Monochrome	Fun	20	Lazy	High
		Trottco	Fun	30	Lazy	High
		Soma Plasma	Fun	45	Lazy	High
	Turn Off	All TVs	Energy	220	Neat	Medium
	Turn On	Monochrome	Fun	18	Lazy	High
		Trottco	Fun	35	Lazy	High
		Soma Plasma	Fun	49	Lazy	High
	Watch TV	Monochrome	Fun	18	Lazy	High
		Trottco	Fun	28	Lazy	High
		Soma Plasma	Fun	42	Lazy	High
VR Glasses	Play	N/A	Fun	60	Playful	High

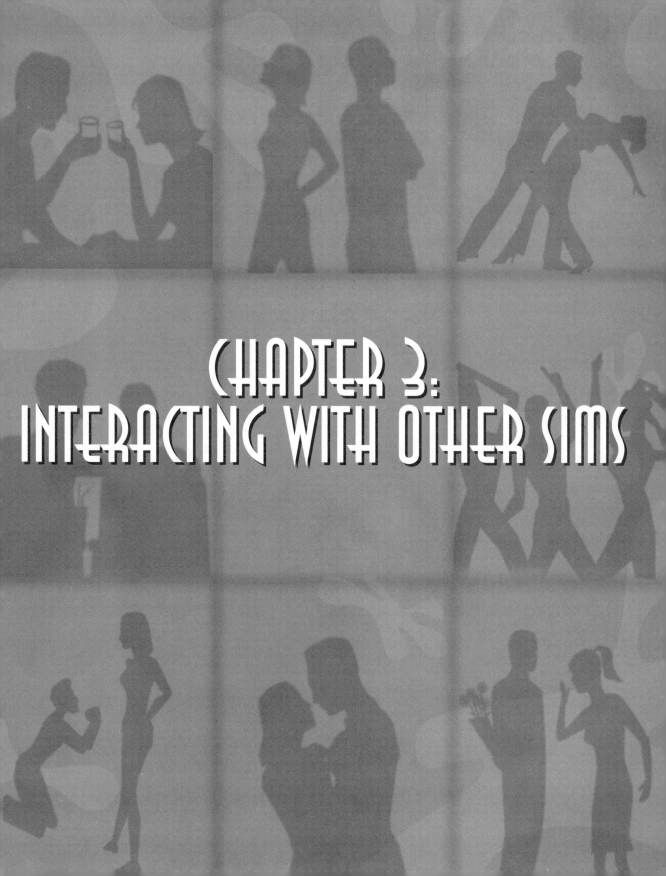

CHAPTER 3:
INTERACTING WITH OTHER SIMS

Introduction

Once you get beyond the dark attraction of watching jilted Sims slap their rivals, or obnoxious Sims insulting their friends, you realize that Relationships are very important to your Sims' quality of life, and even to the advancement of their careers. In this chapter, we introduce you to the world of Relationships, covering the possible events that occur when two Sims come together verbally or physically. Our goal here is to lay down the ground rules. We'll offer hands-on tips for building and maintaining Relationships in the "All in the Family" chapter.

Relationship Scores

Icons representing a Sim's friendships, or lack thereof, appear in the screen's lower-right corner when you click on the Relationships icon (just above the Job icon). The scoring system ranges from below 0 (not good) to 100, which is reserved for one or more significant others. A relationship is considered a true friendship if the score climbs above 50. Only these Relationships are considered when the game calculates career advancements. Consult the next chapter, "9 to 5: Climbing the Career Ladder," for more information on promotion requirements.

Social Interactions

All Sim Relationships develop from Social interactions. If you don't spend quality time with your friends, the Relationships will deteriorate on their own, at a rate of two points per day. Of course, if you interact poorly, the rate accelerates dramatically. In the following sections, we review the myriad communication choices that are available during the game (grouped alphabetically by the active action). At any given time, your choice will vary, depending upon the level of your friendship, and whether or not your Sim is acting like a jerk!

Good Old Conversation

The easiest way to cultivate a new friendship is to talk. Sims communicate with each either using Sim-Speak, a delightful chatter that you actually begin to understand (yes, we have played this game way too much!). Adults and kids have favorite topics within their peer groups. These topics are randomly assigned by the game during the Sim creation process. Additionally, kids and adults have special cross-generational topics that are only used with each other. Active topics are displayed in thought balloons during the game, as shown in figure 3-2.

Fig. 3-1. This Sim Dad is clicking on all cylinders with his wife, but he needs to spend more time with the kids.

Fig. 3-2. Pets are a good common ground for conversation between adults and kids.

When a conversation is going well, you see a green plus sign over one or both of the Sims. Conversely, when talk deteriorates into the gutter, you'll see red minus signs. The following tables list positive and negative communications, including each potential outcome and the corresponding effect on Social and Relationship scores. For our purposes, an outcome is positive if it produces an increase in one or both scores. When scores drop or stay the same, it is considered a negative outcome.

Fig. 3-3. When two or more people enter a hot tub, the conversations begin spontaneously.

Positive Communications

INTERACTION	RESPONSE	RELATIONSHIP CHANGE	SOCIAL SCORE CHANGE
Apologize	Accept	10	15
Be Apologized To	Accept	10	15
Brag	Good	5	13
Be Bragged To	Good	5	7
Cheer Up	Good	5	7
Cheer Up	Neutral	0	5
Be Cheered Up	Good	10	10
Be Cheered Up	Neutral	0	5
Compliment	Accept	5	5
Be Complimented	Accept	5	11
Entertain	Laugh	4	7
Be Entertained	Laugh	8	13
Flirt	Good	5	13
Be Flirted With	Good	10	13
Joke	Laugh	5	13
Joke	Giggle	2	7
Listen to Joke	Laugh	7	13
Listen to Joke	Giggle	3	7
Scare	Laugh	5	10
TalkHigh Interest	Topic	3	5
TalkLike	Topic	3	5
Group Talk	N/A	1	8
Tease	Giggle	5	7

Negative Communications

INTERACTION	RESPONSE	RELATIONSHIP CHANGE	SOCIAL SCORE CHANGE
Apologize	Reject	-10	0
Be Apologized To	Reject	-10	0
Brag	Bad	-5	0
Be Bragged To	Bad	-5	0
Cheer Up	Bad	-3	0
Be Cheered Up	Bad	-10	0
Compliment	Reject	-10	0
Be Complimented	Reject	-7	0
Entertain	Boo	-15	0
Be Entertained	Boo	-7	0
Flirt	Refuse	-10	-17
Flirt	Ignore	-5	0
Be Flirted With	Refuse	-10	0
Be Flirted With	Ignore	0	0
Insult	Cry	5	0
Insult	Stoic	0	3
Insult	Angry	-10	7
Be Insulted	Cry	-12	-13
Be Insulted	Stoic	-5	-5
Be Insulted	Angry	-14	-7
Joke	Uninterested	-6	0
Listen to Joke	Uninterested	-7	0
Scare	Angry	-5	0
Be Scared	Angry	-10	0
TalkDislike	Topic	-3	3
TalkHate	Topic	-3	3
Tease	Cry	-4	0
Be Teased	Cry	-13	-7

Physical Contact

When a Relationship moves past the 50-point threshold, you begin to see new options on the Social interaction menu. Instead of just talking, you find new items including Hug, Give Back Rub, Flirt, and Kiss. It all depends upon how your Relationship is progressing and what the other Sim is looking for in the current interaction. The following tables include information on positive and negative physical events.

Positive Physical Events

INTERACTION	RESPONSE	RELATIONSHIP CHANGE	SOCIAL SCORE CHANGE
Give Back Rub	Good	5	7
Receive Back Rub	Good	9	13
Dance	Accept	8	13
Be Danced With	Accept	10	13
Give Gift	Accept	5	7
Receive Gift	Accept	10	13
Hug	Good	7	15
Hug	Tentative	2	7
Be Hugged	Good	8	15
Be Hugged	Tentative	4	7
Kiss	Passion	12	20
Kiss	Polite	5	10
Be Kissed	Passion	12	20
Be Kissed	Polite	5	10
Tickle	Accept	5	13
Be Tickled	Accept	8	13

Negative Physical Events

INTERACTION	RESPONSE	RELATIONSHIP CHANGE	SOCIAL SCORE CHANGE
Attack	Win Fight	-5	10
Attack	Lose Fight	-10	-20
Give Back Rub	Bad	-7	0
Receive Back Rub	Bad	-10	0
Dance	Refuse	-5	0
Be Danced With	Refuse	-5	0
Give Gift	Stomp	-15	0
Receive Gift	Stomp	-5	0
Hug	Refuse	-10	0
Be Hugged	Refuse	-10	0
Kiss	Deny	-15	5
Be Kissed	Deny	-10	0
Slap	Cry	0	3
Slap	Slap Back	-10	-7
Be Slapped	Cry	-20	-17
Be Slapped	Slap Back	-15	7
Tickle	Refuse	-5	0
Be Tickled	Refuse	-8	0

CHAPTER 4:
9 TO 5—CLIMBING THE CAREER LADDER

Introduction

When you first start playing *The Sims*, it's easy to get lost in the element. There's so much to explore and experience, and with more than enough money to furnish your house and buy a few toys, you can just hang out and live the good Sim-life. But, reality sets in sooner than you would like, and you must find a job. In this chapter we show you how to select a career, nurture the Skills necessary to earn the first few promotions, and finally, stockpile enough friends (it's called networking) to make the big bucks and zoom to the top of your field. For easy reference, we include comprehensive career tables that contain everything you need to know about the 10 Sim careers, including advancement requirements for all 10 pay levels.

Your First Job

Every Sim house receives a daily copy of the *Sim City Times* that includes a single job posting. You can take the first job you see, or buy a computer and view three jobs a day. There is no rush—you have enough money to get by for several days.

TIP

You can enjoy the free use of a computer by buying it, checking the want ads, and then returning it the same day for a full refund. Keep this up until you find the job you want. Then, later when you have more disposable cash, you can buy—and keep—a computer.

A Military job is usually available on the computer. This is an excellent first career, with a starting salary of §250. Furthermore, it remains the highest paying of the 10 careers through the first three advances. A Law Enforcement position is a close second.

Fig. 4-2. This two-commando family takes home §325 each as members of the Elite Forces (Level 2—Military Career).

If you would rather take your time and sort through all 10 job tracks, the following table will help you choose a career that is suited to your Sim's personality traits.

Fig. 4-1. Today's job posting is for a test driver.

Career Choices

CAREER TRACK	NECESSARY SKILLS	RELATED PERSONALITY TRAITS
Business	Logic, Charisma	Outgoing
Entertainment	Charisma, Creativity	Outgoing, Playful
Law Enforcement	Logic, Body	Active
Life of Crime	Creativity, Charisma	Playful, Outgoing
Medicine	Logic, Body	Active
Military	Repair, Body	Active
Politics	Charisma, Logic	Outgoing
Pro Athlete	Body, Charisma	Active, Outgoing
Science	Logic, Creativity	Playful
Xtreme	Creativity, Body/Charisma (tie)	Playful, Active, Outgoing

Developing Your Skills

After you decide on a career, focus on developing the appropriate Skills needed for advancement. It is important to remember that Sims do not study on their own. You need to direct your Sim to one of the activities listed in the Skill Enhancement table below.

On the control panel, click on the Job icon to display your Sim's current Skill bars (see figure 4-3). A white line designates the minimum level of Skill needed for the next promotion. Other factors contribute to earning a promotion, but without the Skill requirement, you have absolutely no chance for advancement to the next level.

Fig. 4-3. This Sim needs to boost his Body Skill one more notch, so he is scheduled for a session on the exercise machine right after lunch.

Skill Enhancement

SKILL	METHOD OF ENHANCEMENT	NOTES
Cooking	Bookshelf (Study Cooking)	Any type of bookshelf will suffice.
Mechanical	Bookshelf (Study Mechanical)	Any type of bookshelf will suffice.
Body	Exercise Machine (Work Out)	Exercise machine increases Skill four times faster than the pool. Active Sims improve their Skill at a higher rate.
	Pool (Swim)	See above.
Charisma	Mirrors or Medicine Cabinet (Practice Speech)	Outgoing Sims acquire Skill more quickly.
	Easel (Paint)	Playful Sims acquire Skill more quickly.
	Piano (Play)	Playful Sims acquire Skill more quickly.
Logic	Chessboard (Play)	Playing with another Sim generates Social points.

Fig. 4-4. A session on the exercise bench nets a Body point for this Sim.

Sim Career Tracks

The following tables include the salaries, hours, car pool vehicles, and job level requirements for each level of the 10 Sim career tracks. The Daily Motive Decay value shows which Motives deteriorate while the Sim is on the job.

Requirements for Level 1 Positions

CAREER TRACK	POSITION	PAY	HOURS	CAR POOL VEHICLE	COOKING	REPAIR	CHARISMA	BODY	LOGIC	CREATIVITY	FAMILY/ FRIENDS	DAILY MOTIVE DECAY						
												HUNGER	COMFORT	HYGIENE	BLADDER	ENERGY	FUN	SOCIAL
Business	Mail Room	§120	9 a.m. –3 p.m.	Junker	0	0	0	0	0	0	0	0	0	0	0	-30	0	0
Entertainment	Waiter Waitress	§100	9 a.m. –3 p.m.	Junker	0	0	0	0	0	0	0	0	0	0	0	-30	0	0
Law Enforcement	Security Guard	§240	12 a.m. –6 a.m.	Squad Car	0	0	0	0	0	0	0	0	0	0	0	-30	0	0
Life of Crime	Pickpocket	§140	9 a.m. –3 p.m.	Junker	0	0	0	0	0	0	0	0	0	0	0	-30	0	0
Medicine	Medical Technician	§200	9 a.m. –3 p.m.	Junker	0	0	0	0	0	0	0	0	0	0	0	-30	0	0
Military	Recruit	§250	6 a.m. –12 p.m.	Military Jeep	0	0	0	0	0	0	0	0	0	-15	0	-30	0	0
Politics	Campaign Work	§220	9 a.m. –6 p.m.	Junker	0	0	0	0	0	0	0	0	0	0	0	-30	0	0
Pro Athlete	Team Mascot	§110	12 a.m. –6 p.m.	Junker	0	0	0	0	0	0	0	0	0	-5	0	-35	0	0
Science	Test Subject	§155	9 a.m. –3 p.m.	Junker	0	0	0	0	0	0	0	0	0	0	0	-30	0	0
Xtreme	Daredevil	§175	9 a.m. –3 p.m.	Junker	0	0	0	0	0	0	0	0	0	0	0	-30	0	0

Requirements for Level 2 Positions

CAREER TRACK	POSITION	PAY	HOURS	CAR POOL VEHICLE	COOKING	REPAIR	CHARISMA	BODY	LOGIC	CREATIVITY	FAMILY/ FRIENDS	DAILY MOTIVE DECAY						
												HUNGER	COMFORT	HYGIENE	BLADDER	ENERGY	FUN	SOCIAL
Business	Executive Assistant	§180	9 a.m. –4 p.m	Junker	0	0	0	0	0	0	0	0	0	0	0	-34	-2	0
Entertainment	Extra	§150	9 a.m. –3 p.m.	Junker	0	0	0	0	0	0	0	0	0	0	0	-34	-2	0
Law Enforcement	Cadet	§320	9 a.m. –3 p.m.	Squad Car	0	0	0	0	0	0	0	0	0	0	0	-34	-2	0
Life of Crime	Bagman	§200	11 p.m. –7 a.m.	Junker	0	0	0	0	0	0	0	0	0	0	0	-34	-2	0
Medicine	Paramedic	§275	11 p.m. –5 a.m.	Junker	0	0	0	0	0	0	0	0	0	0	0	-34	-2	0
Military	Elite Forces	§325	7 a.m. –1 p.m.	Military Jeep	0	0	0	0	0	0	0	0	0	-15	0	-34	-2	0
Politics	Intern	§300	9 a.m. –3 p.m.	Junker	0	0	0	0	0	0	0	0	0	0	0	-34	-2	0
Pro Athlete	Minor Leaguer	§170	9 a.m. –3 p.m.	Junker	0	0	0	0	0	0	0	0	0	-10	0	-40	-2	0
Science	Lab Assistant	§230	11 p.m. –5 a.m.	Junker	0	0	0	0	0	0	0	0	0	0	0	-34	-2	0
Xtreme	Bungee Jump Instructor	§250	9 a.m. –3 p.m.	Junker	0	0	0	0	0	0	0	0	0	0	0	-34	-2	0

Requirements for Level 3 Positions

CAREER TRACK	POSITION	PAY	HOURS	CAR POOL VEHICLE	COOKING	REPAIR	CHARISMA	BODY	LOGIC	CREATIVITY	FAMILY/ FRIENDS	DAILY MOTIVE DECAY						
												HUNGER	COMFORT	HYGIENE	BLADDER	ENERGY	FUN	SOCIAL
Business	Field Sales Rep	§250	9 a.m.–4 p.m.	Junker	0	2	0	0	0	0	0	-3	0	-5	0	-38	-4	0
Entertainment	Bit Player	§200	9 a.m.–3 p.m.	Junker	0	0	2	0	0	0	0	-3	0	-5	0	-38	-4	0
Law Enforcement	Patrol Officer	§380	5 p.m.–1 a.m.	Squad Car	0	0	0	2	0	0	0	-3	0	-5	0	-38	-4	0
Life of Crime	Bookie	§275	12 p.m.–7 p.m.	Standard Car	0	0	0	2	0	0	0	-3	0	-5	0	-38	-4	0
Medicine	Nurse	§340	9 a.m.–3 p.m.	Standard Car	0	2	0	0	0	0	0	-3	0	-5	0	-38	-4	0
Military	Drill Instructor	§250	8 a.m.–2 p.m.	Military Jeep	0	0	0	2	0	0	0	-3	0	-20	0	-38	-4	0
Politics	Lobbyist	§360	9 a.m.–3 p.m.	Standard Car	0	0	2	0	0	0	0	-3	0	-5	0	-38	-4	0
Pro Athlete	Rookie	§230	9 a.m.–3 p.m.	Junker	0	0	0	2	0	0	0	-3	0	-15	0	-45	-2	0
Science	Field Researcher	§320	9 a.m.–3 p.m.	Standard Car	0	0	0	0	2	0	0	-3	0	-5	0	-38	-4	0
Xtreme	Whitewater Guide	§325	9 a.m.–3 p.m.	SUV	0	0	0	2	0	0	1	-3	0	-10	0	-45	-4	0

Requirements for Level 4 Positions

CAREER TRACK	POSITION	PAY	HOURS	CAR POOL VEHICLE	COOKING	REPAIR	CHARISMA	BODY	LOGIC	CREATIVITY	FAMILY/ FRIENDS	DAILY MOTIVE DECAY						
												HUNGER	COMFORT	HYGIENE	BLADDER	ENERGY	FUN	SOCIAL
Business	Junior Executive	§320	9 a.m.–4 p.m.	Standard Car	0	2	2	0	0	0	1	-7	0	-10	0	-42	-7	0
Entertainment	Stunt Double	§275	9 a.m.–4 p.m.	Standard Car	0	0	2	2	0	0	2	-7	0	-10	0	-42	-7	0
Law Enforcement	Desk Sergeant	§440	9 a.m.–3 p.m.	Squad Car	0	2	0	2	0	0	1	-7	0	-10	0	-42	-7	0
Life of Crime	Con Artist	§350	9 a.m.–3 p.m.	Standard Car	0	0	1	2	0	1	2	-7	0	-10	0	-42	-7	0
Medicine	Intern	§410	9 a.m.–6 p.m.	Standard Car	0	2	0	2	0	0	2	-7	0	-10	0	-42	-7	0
Military	Junior Officer	§450	9 a.m.–3 p.m.	Military Jeep	0	1	2	2	0	0	0	-7	0	-20	0	-42	-8	0
Politics	Campaign Manager	§430	9 a.m.–6 p.m.	Standard Car	0	0	2	0	1	0	2	-7	0	-10	0	-42	-7	0
Pro Athlete	Starter	§300	9 a.m.–3 p.m.	Standard Car	0	0	0	5	0	0	1	-7	0	-20	0	-50	-2	0
Science	Science Teacher	§375	9 a.m.–4 p.m.	Standard Car	0	0	1	0	3	0	1	-7	0	-10	0	-40	-7	0
Xtreme	Xtreme Circuit Pro	§400	9 a.m.–3 p.m.	SUV	0	1	0	4	0	0	2	-7	0	-20	0	-50	-2	0

Requirements for Level 5 Positions

CAREER TRACK	POSITION	PAY	HOURS	CAR POOL VEHICLE	COOKING	REPAIR	CHARISMA	BODY	LOGIC	CREATIVITY	FAMILY/ FRIENDS	DAILY MOTIVE DECAY						
												HUNGER	COMFORT	HYGIENE	BLADDER	ENERGY	FUN	SOCIAL
Business	Executive	§400	9 a.m.–4 p.m.	Standard Car	0	2	2	0	2	0	3	-10	0	-15	0	-46	-10	0
Entertainment	B-Movie Star	§375	10 a.m.–5 p.m.	Standard Car	0	0	3	3	0	1	4	-10	0	-15	0	-46	-10	0
Law Enforcement	Vice Squad	§490	10 p.m.–4 a.m.	Squad Car	0	3	0	4	0	0	2	-10	0	-15	0	-46	-10	0
Life of Crime	Getaway Driver	§425	5 p.m.–1 a.m.	Standard Car	0	2	1	2	0	2	3	-10	0	-10	0	-46	-10	0
Medicine	Resident	§480	9 p.m.–4 a.m.	Standard Car	0	3	0	2	2	0	3	-10	0	-15	0	-46	-10	0
Military	Counter-Intelligence	§500	9 a.m.–3 p.m.	Military Jeep	1	1	2	4	0	0	0	-10	0	-25	0	-46	-12	0
Politics	City Council Member	§485	9 a.m.–3 p.m.	Town Car	0	0	3	1	1	0	4	-10	0	-15	0	-46	-8	0
Pro Athlete	All-Star	§385	9 a.m.–3 p.m.	SUV	0	1	1	6	0	0	3	-10	0	-25	0	-55	-3	0
Science	Project Leader	§450	9 a.m.–5 p.m.	Standard Car	0	0	2	0	4	1	3	-10	0	-12	0	-43	-8	0
Xtreme	Bush Pilot	§475	9 a.m.–3 p.m.	SUV	1	2	0	4	1	0	3	-10	0	-15	0	-46	-5	-10

Requirements for Level 6 Positions

CAREER TRACK	POSITION	PAY	HOURS	CAR POOL VEHICLE	COOKING	REPAIR	CHARISMA	BODY	LOGIC	CREATIVITY	FAMILY/ FRIENDS	DAILY MOTIVE DECAY						
												HUNGER	COMFORT	HYGIENE	BLADDER	ENERGY	FUN	SOCIAL
Business	Senior Manager	§520	9 a.m.–4 p.m.	Standard Car	0	2	3	0	3	2	6	-14	0	-20	0	-50	-13	0
Entertainment	Supporting Player	§500	10 a.m.–6 p.m.	Limo	0	1	4	4	0	2	6	-14	0	-20	0	-50	-13	0
Law Enforcement	Detective	§540	9 a.m.–3 p.m.	Squad Car	1	3	1	5	1	0	4	-14	0	-20	0	-50	-13	0
Life of Crime	Bank Robber	§530	3 p.m.–11 p.m.	Town Car	0	3	2	3	1	2	4	-14	0	-15	0	-50	-13	-5
Medicine	GP	§550	10 a.m.–6 p.m.	Town Car	0	3	1	3	4	0	4	-14	0	-20	0	-50	-13	0
Military	Flight Officer	§550	9 a.m.–3 p.m.	Military Jeep	1	2	4	4	1	0	1	-14	0	-28	0	-50	-15	0
Politics	State Assemblyperson	§540	9 a.m.–4 p.m.	Town Car	0	0	4	2	1	1	6	-14	0	-20	0	-50	-12	-3
Pro Athlete	MVP	§510	9 a.m.–3 p.m.	SUV	0	2	2	7	0	0	5	-14	0	-30	0	-60	-4	0
Science	Inventor	§540	10 a.m.–7 p.m.	Town Car	0	2	2	0	4	3	4	-14	0	-15	0	-45	-9	-8
Xtreme	Mountain Climber	§550	9 a.m.–3 p.m.	SUV	1	4	0	6	1	0	4	-14	0	-30	0	-60	0	0

Requirements for Level 7 Positions

CAREER TRACK	POSITION	PAY	HOURS	CAR POOL VEHICLE	COOKING	REPAIR	CHARISMA	BODY	LOGIC	CREATIVITY	FAMILY/ FRIENDS	DAILY MOTIVE DECAY						
												HUNGER	COMFORT	HYGIENE	BLADDER	ENERGY	FUN	SOCIAL
Business	Vice President	§660	9 a.m. –5 p.m.	Town Car	0	2	4	2	4	2	8	-18	0	-25	0	-54	-16	0
Entertainment	TV Star	§650	10 a.m. –6 p.m.	Limo	0	1	6	5	0	3	8	-18	0	-25	0	-54	-16	0
Law Enforcement	Lieutenant	§590	9 a.m. –3 p.m.	Limo	1	3	2	5	3	1	6	-18	0	-25	0	-54	-16	0
Life of Crime	Cat Burglar	§640	9 p.m. –3 a.m.	Town Car	1	3	2	5	2	3	6	-18	0	-20	0	-54	-16	0
Medicine	Specialist	§625	10 p.m. –4 a.m.	Town Car	0	4	2	4	4	1	5	-18	0	-25	0	-54	-16	0
Military	Senior Officer	§580	9 a.m. –3 p.m.	Military Jeep	1	3	4	5	3	0	3	-18	0	-31	0	-55	-20	0
Politics	Congress-person	§600	9 a.m. –3 p.m.	Town Car	0	0	4	3	3	2	9	-18	0	-25	0	-54	-18	-7
Pro Athlete	Superstar	§680	9 a.m. –4 p.m.	SUV	1	2	3	8	0	0	7	-18	0	-35	0	-65	-5	0
Science	Scholar	§640	10 a.m. –3 p.m.	Town Car	0	4	2	0	6	4	5	-18	0	-20	0	-48	-10	-10
Xtreme	Photo-journalist	§650	9 a.m. –3 p.m.	SUV	1	5	2	6	1	3	5	-18	0	-25	0	-54	-16	0

Requirements for Level 8 Positions

CAREER TRACK	POSITION	PAY	HOURS	CAR POOL VEHICLE	COOKING	REPAIR	CHARISMA	BODY	LOGIC	CREATIVITY	FAMILY/ FRIENDS	DAILY MOTIVE DECAY						
												HUNGER	COMFORT	HYGIENE	BLADDER	ENERGY	FUN	SOCIAL
Business	President	§800	9 a.m. –5 p.m.	Town Car	0	2	5	2	6	3	10	-22	0	-30	0	-58	-19	0
Entertainment	Feature Star	§900	5 p.m. –1 a.m.	Limo	0	2	7	6	0	4	10	-22	0	-30	0	-58	-19	0
Law Enforcement	SWAT Team Leader	§625	9 a.m. –3 p.m.	Limo	1	4	3	6	5	1	8	-22	0	-30	0	-58	-19	0
Life of Crime	Counterfeiter	§760	9 p.m. –3 a.m.	Town Car	1	5	2	5	3	5	8	-22	0	-25	0	-58	-19	-15
Medicine	Surgeon	§700	10 p.m. –4 a.m.	Town Car	0	4	3	5	6	2	7	-22	0	-30	0	-58	-19	0
Military	Commander	§600	9 a.m. –3 p.m.	Military Jeep	1	6	5	5	5	0	5	-22	0	-33	0	-60	-25	0
Politics	Judge	§650	9 a.m. –3 p.m.	Town Car	0	0	5	4	4	3	11	-22	0	-30	0	-58	-22	-11
Pro Athlete	Assistant Coach	§850	9 a.m. –2 p.m.	SUV	2	2	4	9	0	1	9	-22	0	-40	0	-70	-6	0
Science	Top Secret Researcher	§740	10 a.m. –3 p.m.	Town Car	1	6	4	0	7	4	7	-22	0	-25	0	-52	-12	-13
Xtreme	Treasure Hunter	§725	10 a.m. –5 p.m.	SUV	1	6	3	7	3	4	7	-22	0	-34	0	-60	-15	-5

Requirements for Level 9 Positions

CAREER TRACK	POSITION	PAY	HOURS	CAR POOL VEHICLE	COOKING	REPAIR	CHARISMA	BODY	LOGIC	CREATIVITY	FAMILY/ FRIENDS	DAILY MOTIVE DECAY						
												HUNGER	COMFORT	HYGIENE	BLADDER	ENERGY	FUN	SOCIAL
Business	CEO	§950	9 a.m.–4 p.m.	Limo	0	2	6	2	7	5	12	-26	0	-35	0	-62	-22	0
Entertainment	Broadway Star	§1100	10 a.m.–5 p.m.	Limo	0	2	8	7	0	7	12	-26	0	-35	0	-62	-22	0
Law Enforcement	Police Chief	§650	9 a.m.–5 p.m.	Limo	1	4	4	7	7	3	10	-26	0	-35	0	-62	-22	0
Life of Crime	Smuggler	§900	9 a.m.–3 p.m.	Town Car	1	5	5	6	3	6	10	-26	0	-30	0	-62	-22	-20
Medicine	Medical Researcher	§775	9 p.m.–4 a.m.	Limo	0	5	4	6	8	3	9	-26	0	-35	0	-62	-22	0
Military	Astronaut	§625	9 a.m.–3 p.m.	Limo	1	9	5	8	6	0	6	-26	0	-35	0	-65	-30	0
Politics	Senator	§700	9 a.m.–6 p.m.	Limo	0	0	6	5	6	4	14	-26	0	-35	0	-62	-26	-15
Pro Athlete	Coach	§1,000	9 a.m.–3 p.m.	SUV	3	2	6	10	0	2	11	-26	0	-45	0	-75	-8	0
Science	Theorist	§870	10 a.m.–2 p.m.	Town Car	1	7	4	0	9	7	8	-26	0	-30	0	-56	-16	-16
Xtreme	Grand Prix Driver	§825	10 a.m.–4 p.m.	Bentley	1	6	5	7	5	7	9	-26	0	-35	0	-62	-5	-10

Requirements for Level 10 Positions

CAREER TRACK	POSITION	PAY	HOURS	CAR POOL VEHICLE	COOKING	REPAIR	CHARISMA	BODY	LOGIC	CREATIVITY	FAMILY/ FRIENDS	DAILY MOTIVE DECAY						
												HUNGER	COMFORT	HYGIENE	BLADDER	ENERGY	FUN	SOCIAL
Business	Business Tycoon	§1,200	9 a.m.–3 p.m.	Limo	0	2	8	2	9	6	14	-30	0	-40	0	-66	-25	0
Entertainment	Super-star	§1,400	10 a.m.–3 p.m.	Limo	0	2	10	8	0	10	14	-30	0	-40	0	-66	-25	0
Law Enforcement	Captain Hero	§700	10 a.m.–4 p.m.	Limo	1	4	6	7	10	5	12	-20	-80	-45	-25	-60	0	0
Life of Crime	Criminal Mastermind	§1,100	6 p.m.–12 a.m.	Limo	2	5	7	6	4	8	12	-30	0	-35	0	-66	-25	-25
Medicine	Chief of Staff	§850	9 p.m.–4 a.m.	Hospital Limo	0	6	6	7	9	4	11	-30	0	-40	0	-66	-25	0
Military	General	§650	9 a.m.–3 p.m.	Staff Sedan	1	10	7	10	9	0	8	-30	0	-40	0	-70	-35	0
Politics	Mayor	§750	9 a.m.–3 p.m	Limo	0	0	9	5	7	5	17	-30	0	-40	0	-66	-30	-20
Pro Athlete	Hall of Famer	§1,300	9 a.m.–3 p.m.	Limo	4	2	9	10	0	3	13	-30	0	-50	0	-80	-10	0
Science	Mad Scientist	§1,000	10 a.m.–2 p.m.	Limo	2	8	5	0	10	10	10	-30	0	-35	0	-60	-20	-20
Xtreme	International	§925	11 a.m.–5 p.m.	Bentley	2	6	8	8	6	9	11	-30	0	-30	0	-70	-20	-15

The Daily Grind

A working Sim needs to follow a schedule that is conducive to good job performance. Review the following tips as you devise a work schedule for your household.

Get Plenty of Sleep

Sims need to awake refreshed in order to arrive at work in a good mood. Send your Sims to bed early, and make sure there are no distractions (stereos, TVs, computers, etc.) that might interrupt their beauty sleep.

Fig. 4-5. Make sure your Sims get to bed early enough to restore maximum Energy before the alarm rings.

Set Your Alarm Clock

When set, the clock wakes your Sims two hours before the car pool arrives (one alarm clock takes care of the entire house). This is plenty of time to take care of Hunger, Bladder, and Hygiene Motive bars. If you still have time, improve your Sim's mood with a little non-strenuous fun like watching TV, or use the extra time to improve a Skill.

Fig. 4-6. That last set on the exercise bench paid off!

If two or more Sims in the house have jobs, the alarm clock rings for the earliest riser. Unfortunately, this wakes everyone else, regardless of when they have to be ready for the car pool. If you send the other Sims back to bed, you'll need to wake them manually, because the alarm clock only rings once each day.

Eat a Hearty Breakfast

When you're angling for a promotion, you need to arrive at work with all cylinders firing. When the alarm rings, send the designated house chef (the Sim with the highest Cooking Skill) to the kitchen to "Prepare a Meal." By the time your Sim is finished emptying his Bladder and completing necessary Hygiene, breakfast will be on the counter. There should be plenty of time to complete the meal and head to work with a full Hunger bar.

TIP

Make sure that your Sim is on the first floor and relatively close to the car pool within 15 minutes of departure to be sure he or she catches his or her ride. If you meet this deadline, your Sim will change clothes on the fly and sprint to the curb.

Make Friends and Influence Your Boss

Advancing through the first three levels does not carry a friendship requirement; however this ramps up very quickly. It helps to have a stay-at-home mate to concentrate on making friends. Remember that the career friendship requirement is for your household, not your Sim. So, if your mate or children have friends, they count toward your promotions, too.

Fig. 4-7. This Sim is just about out of Energy, but his Social score is maxed out and he's just made two new friends.

Take an Occasional Day Off to Recharge

If you find that your Sim is unable to have enough Fun or Social events to maintain a positive mood, skip a day of work and indulge. See a friend or two, work on Skills, or have some Fun. Just don't miss two days in a row or your Sim will be automatically fired!

Major Decisions

As you work your way up the career ladder, you encounter "major decisions" that involve various degrees of risk. They are winner-take-all, loser-gets-nada events that force you to gamble with your salary, integrity, or even your job. The following sections include a sample "major decision" for each career.

Business

Major decision: "Stock Option"

Player is given the choice of accepting a portfolio of company stock instead of salary for that pay period. The stock could double or tank. As a result, the player receives twice his salary or nothing at all for the pay period.

Entertainment

Major decision: "The Remake"

Your agent calls with an offer: Sim Studios wants you for the lead in a remake of *Citizen Kane*. Accepting will either send your Charisma sky high when the film succeeds wildly...or send it crashing if the turkey flops.

Law Enforcement

Major decision: "The Bribe"

A mobster you're investigating offers a huge bribe to drop the case. The charges won't stick without your testimony and you *could* suddenly "lose the evidence" and quietly pocket a nice nest egg...or get busted by Internal Affairs and have to start over on a new career track.

Life of Crime

Major decision: "The Perfect Crime"

You've just been handed a hot tip that an informant claims will be an easy knockover with loads of cash for the taking. Either the tip is gold, or it's a police sting. An arrest means your family is left at home alone while you're sent off to cool your heels in Sim City Prison for a while. If you succeed, your Charisma and Creativity Skills are enhanced.

Medicine

Major Decision: "Malpractice"

A former patient has slapped you with a massive malpractice suit. You can settle immediately by offering a payment equal to 50 percent of the cash in your household account. Or, take the bum to court. Lose, and all your furniture and household goods are repossessed. Win, and you receive a settlement equal to 100 percent of the cash in your household account.

Military

Major decision: "Gung Ho"

The general needs volunteers for a highly dangerous mission. You can refuse without penalty. If you accept, and succeed on the mission, you are decorated and immediately promoted to the next level. Failure means a demotion, soldier—you're broken down to the previous level.

Politics

Major decision: "Scandal"

An attractive young member of your team also happens to be heir to a fortune. He or she will finance your career advancement if you agree to "private consultations." You can refuse, with no change in status. Otherwise, there are two possible outcomes. You might get away with it and immediately advance *two* levels. If you're caught, you'll lose your friends when the scandal breaks in the media, and you'll be tossed from the career track to seek another.

Pro Athlete

Major Decision: "The Supermatch"

A one-on-one, pay-per-view contest pitting you against your greatest local rival is offered. If you win, it's worth double your paycheck. If you lose, the indignity comes complete with an injury costing you a reduction in your Body Skill along with a drop in Charisma. The player can always refuse at no penalty.

Science

Major decision: "The Experiment"

A science research firm is willing to pay you a fat bonus for conducting a complex experiment. However, the work must be conducted at your home, using rats as test subjects. Success means you collect the fee, with a bonus increase in your Logic Skill level. A failed experiment results in a dozen rats escaping into your home. That means a major bill from both your exterminator and your electrician (the rats have chewed through power cords.) Financial damage could be reduced if the Player's Repair Skills are strong.

Xtreme

Major decision: "Deep Freeze"

An arctic expedition is holding a spot open for you. It's a risky enterprise, so you may refuse. However, for a person in your particular line of work, that refusal will lower your Charisma. If you join the team, and they reach their goal, you will be rewarded with a considerable rise in Charisma. If the mission goes awry, your Sim is "lost on an iceberg" for a period of game time.

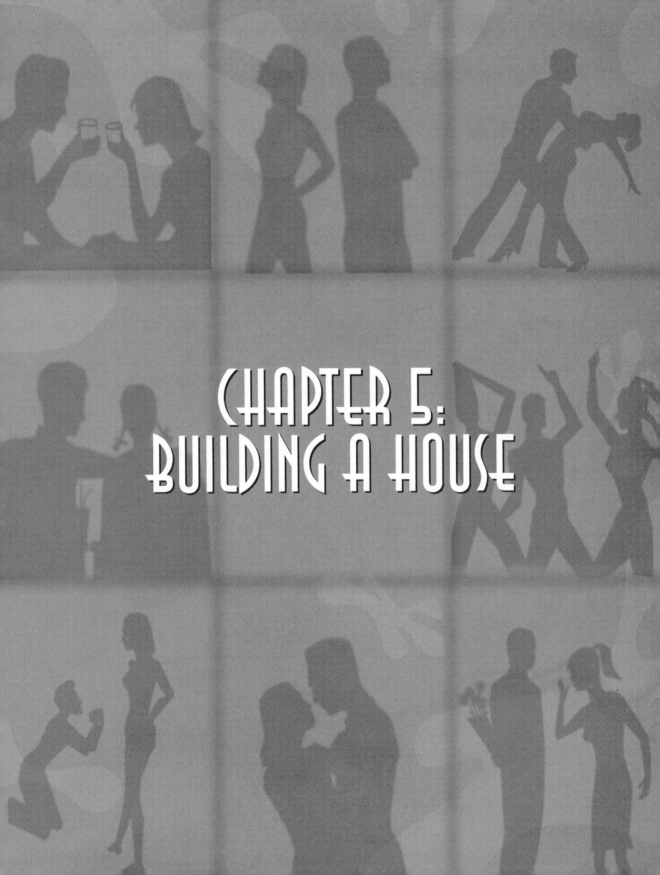

CHAPTER 5: BUILDING A HOUSE

Introduction

Anyone who has ever built a home knows that the best laid plans of architects can sometimes turn into a house of horrors when the walls start going up. The same holds true in *The Sims*, where you have enough power to build a magnificent dream house or your worst residential nightmare. Limited only by your bank account, you can build a conservative dwelling that is functional above all else, or you can drop a family of eight in the middle of a meadow with only a bathroom and a refrigerator. It's all possible in *The Sims*, but rest assured that your family will deliver a quick—and sometimes scathing—critique when the clock starts ticking on their simulated lives.

In this chapter, we take you through the house design process from terrain preparation to landscaping. For demonstration purposes, we will use just about every building option available. Obviously, you would need a pile of Simoleans to do this in the game. However, we also cover important design considerations that enable you to maximize your Room score, regardless of your budget. In this chapter, we limit our discussion to the available options in Build Mode only. For detailed descriptions of more than 150 *Sims* objects, see the next chapter.

Of course, our suggestions are just the beginning. Sims thrive on the individuality of their creator, and if you want to build dungeons, sprawling compounds, or one-room huts, you have our support and encouragement. Remember, a bad house is no match for the bulldozer—your next house is only a click away!

TIP

Don't try to build your dream house at the beginning of the game. It's easier to tear down your original house and start over after you've fattened up your bank account.

Design Considerations

Before we introduce you to the various options available in Build Mode, here is a checklist for your basic floor plan. Invariably, your unique family of Sims will make their needs known to you as the game progresses. However, if you follow these house design basics, you should get your family off to a positive start with a minimum of emotional outbursts.

* **Don't worry about having room to expand. Build your first house to match the number of Sims in your family.**
* **Keep the bathroom centrally located. A door on either side allows quick access for emergencies.**
* **If you start with three Sims or more, build one or more half-bathrooms (toilet and sink only) to ease the crunch.**
* **Place the house close to the street, so you don't have to do the hundred yard dash to meet your car pool.**
* **Allow enough open wall for your kitchen countertops and appliances.**
* **Make your kitchen large enough to accommodate a small table and chairs.**
* **If you don't want a separate den or family room, make one of the bedrooms large enough to handle a computer desk and chair.**

Terrain Tools

In most locations, you can build a roomy house on a flat piece of land without having to level the terrain. However, if you want to build a house near the water or at the edge of a hill, you'll need to smooth the sloping tiles before building a wall, as displayed in figure 5-1.

Fig. 5-1. You can't place a wall section until you smooth the slope.

The Terrain Tool (shovel icon) can be a little tricky to master. On level ground, you can place the shovel at any intersection of horizontal and vertical grid lines, and then click to level, lower, or raise the tile. However, sometimes, due to extreme depth or elevation (usually at the edge of a gully or alongside water), you can't access this intersecting point. When this occurs, you receive a message telling you that the tile cannot be modified (figure 5-2).

TIP

The grid lines become noticeably darker when a previously elevated or lowered tile becomes level.

Fig. 5–2. You cannot level a tile at the water's edge.

In most cases, there is no need to edit the terrain, unless you want to add a sunken hot tub or drop an outdoor play set into a pit. Remember that you must level the ground in the pit before you can place an object (see figure 5-3).

Fig. 5-3. You cannot place the play set until the tiles in the pit are level.

Wall and Fence Tools

There are several tools here, but your first step is to "frame" your house. Simply place the cursor at any tile intersection. Then click, hold, and drag to place your wall (figure 5-4). When you release the mouse button, the wood framing will change to the type of wall you selected on the Control Panel (see page 52 for descriptions of wall types).

Fig. 5-4. Drag and release to place a wall.

Although you must start a wall at an intersection, you are not limited to square walls. Simply drag the cursor at an angle to create an interesting corner (figure 5-5). However, don't make the angled walls too long. You cannot place doors, windows, or objects on these walls. Also, you cannot connect an angled wall to an existing straight wall inside your house.

To delete a wall, hold down the Ctrl *key, then click and drag on a section of wall.*

Fig. 5-5. Angled corners help you transform a boring box into a custom home.

Don't worry if you end up with a tree inside the walls of your house. You can build an atrium and keep the tree where it is, or use the Hand Tool to select the tree, and then move or delete it.

Wall Tool

Wall Types

NAME	COST (PER SECTION)	DESCRIPTION
White Picket Fence	§10	Outdoor fencing
Privacy Fence	§35	8-foot outdoor fence
Monticello Balustrade	§45	Railings for balconies and stairs
Wrought Iron Balustrade	§45	Railings for balconies and stairs
Tumbleweed Wooden Column	§70	Support columns for second stories or patio covers
Wall Tool	§70	Basic unfinished wall
The Zorba Ionic Column	§80	Classic, white Graeco-Roman column
Chester Brick Column	§100	All brick, squared off column

Columns are not restricted to outside use. Try using the Zorba Ionic Column to create a beautiful entry from the living room into a formal dining room.

Door and Window Tools

Door Tool

Sims are very active. They seek the best path for their current task, and they think nothing of going out one exterior door and back in through another, if it's the best route. The least expensive Walnut Door (figure 5-6) is only §100, but because it is solid, your Room score does not benefit from outside light. If at all possible, invest in one of the windowed doors, and ideally, pick the multi-paned Monticello Door for maximum light.

Fig. 5-6. The Walnut Door gives your Sims privacy, but it doesn't allow outside light to improve your Room score.

Door Types

NAME	COST	NOTES
Walnut Door	§100	Solid door without windows
Maple Door Frame	§150	Wooden door frame for rooms that do not require total privacy
Federal Lattice Window Door	§200	Glass panes in the upper half of door
Windsor Door	§300	Designer leaded glass door
Monticello Door	§400	7 rows of 3 panes, topped with a 6-pane half circle, allow maximum light to flow into your home

Window Tool

Let the sun shine in to pump up your Room score. Sims love light, so install plenty of windows from the start. Simply click on the selected window and place it on any right-angle wall (remember, you cannot place doors, windows, or objects on a diagonal wall). Window style is strictly personal—all windows exert the same positive effect on the Room score.

For aesthetic value, match your windows to your door style, such as the Monticello Door with Monticello Windows, as pictured in figure 5-7.

Fig. 5-7. Monticello Doors and Windows provide maximum light.

Window Types

NAME	COST	DESCRIPTION
Single-Pane Fixed Window	§50	This economy window still lets in the sun.
Single-Hung Window	§55	This looks good over the kitchen sink.
Privacy Window	§60	Tired of the neighborhood peeping Toms? This window is positioned higher on the wall.
Plate Glass Window	§65	This one's strictly glass from floor to ceiling.
El Sol Window	§80	This round ornamental window is a nice change from square and rectangular styles.
Monticello Window	§110	Use as a bedroom window to complement the Monticello door.
Windsor Window	§120	This ornamental natural wood window adds turn-of-the-century character to your home.
Monticello Window Full-Length	§200	This dramatic window looks beautiful on either side of a Monticello door.

Floor Tool

Unless you like grass in your living room, use the Floor Tool to lay some flooring inside your house. *The Sims* also includes outdoor flooring that works well in patios, backyard barbecue areas, or as pathways to a pool or play area. One tile covers a single grid, and you can quickly finish an entire room with a single shift-click. The price range for floor coverings is §10–§20, and you have a selection of 29 different styles/colors.

TIP

When you lay flooring inside a room with angled walls, half of the floor tiles appear on the other side of the wall, in another room or outside the house (see figure 5-8). To remove these outside tiles, place any floor type over the tiles, hold down the Ctrl *key, and then click to delete them. The flooring on the other side of the wall remains undisturbed.*

Fig. 5-8. After you finish the inside flooring, go back and delete the external tiles.

NOTE

You can use any type of flooring inside or outside.

Flooring Types

- **Carpeting (7)**
- **Cement (1)**
- **Ceramic Tile-Small Tiles (3)**
- **Checkerboard Linoleum (1)**
- **Clay Paver Tiles (1)**
- **Colored Pavement (1)**
- **Granite (2)**
- **Gravel (1)**
- **Hardwood Plank (1)**
- **Inlaid Hardwood (1)**
- **Italian Tile (1)**
- **Poured Concrete (1)**
- **Shale (1)**
- **Striped Pavement (2, Both Directions)**
- **Tatami Mats (2)**
- **Terracotta Tile (1)**
- **Wood Parquet (2)**

Wallpaper Tool

Fig. 5-9. Use the Wallpaper Tool to create a different mood in every room.

There are 30 different indoor/outdoor wall coverings in *The Sims,* and just as with floor coverings, you are limited only by your budget and sense of style. Prices range from §4 for basic wallpaper to §14 for granite block. If you change your mind after putting up the wallpaper, you can rip it down and get your money back by holding down the Ctrl key and clicking on the ugly panel.

Wallpaper Types

- **Adobe (1)**
- **Aluminum Siding (1)**
- **Brick (2)**
- **Granite (1)**
- **Interior Wall Treatments (6 Fabric and Paint Combinations)**
- **Japanese Paper/Screens (4)**
- **Paint (4)**
- **Plaster (1)**
- **Stucco (1)**
- **Tudor (1)**
- **Wainscoting (1)**
- **Wallpaper (4)**
- **Wood Clapboard (1)**
- **Wood Paneling (1)**
- **Wood Shingles (1)**

Stair Tool

You may not plan to build a second story immediately, but it's still a good idea to place your staircase before you start filling your house with objects. Choose from four staircases, two at §900 and two at §1,200. But, no matter how much you spend, they still get your Sims up and down the same way.

Style is considerably less important than function. You don't want to interrupt the traffic flow inside your house, especially to critical rooms such as the bathroom and kitchen. For this reason, staircases work well against a wall, where they are out of the way, or between two large, open rooms, such as the kitchen and family room (figure 5-10).

Fig. 5-11. Our house has a Steep Pitch with dark roof tiles.

Fig. 5-10. Both of these placements keep the staircases out of the main traffic patterns.

If you don't have the money to finish the second story, just place the staircase and forget about it. The Sims won't go upstairs until you add a second story. After the staircase is positioned, the process for building a second story is exactly the same as building the first floor. The only obvious difference is that the buildable wall space extends out one square beyond the walls on the first floor. This allows you to squeeze a little extra space for a larger room or balcony.

Roof Tool

Although it is much easier to play The Sims using the Walls Cutaway or Walls Down options on the Control Panel, you will want to step back and enjoy your masterpiece in all of its crowning glory. The Roof Tool allows you to select a Shallow, Medium, or Steep Pitch for your roof, and choose from a selection of four roof patterns.

Water Tools

Now that you have walls, floors, and doors, it's time to add a pool. Of course, this isn't a necessity, but your Sims love to swim, and it's an easy way to add important Body points. After placing your pool, don't forget to add a diving board so your Sims can get in, and a ladder so they can climb out. As you build your pool, the Water Tool places light-colored cement squares as decking. You can go back and cover these tiles with the outdoor surface of your choice, as displayed in figure 5-12. You can also add fencing around your deck to give your pool a more finished look.

Fig. 5-12. With the pool and decking in place, you have room to add an outdoor barbecue and beverage cart.

Fireplace Tool

Fig. 5-13. It looks innocent enough, but a roaring fire can turn nearby objects or Sims into a deadly inferno.

When placed safely out of the way of flammable objects, a fireplace adds a major boost to the Room score. However, it can be a dangerous fire hazard if Sims wander too close, so give it a wide berth when a fire is roaring.

Plant Tool

Now, it's time to put the finishing touches on the exterior of your house. Using the Plant Tool, you can select from 14 different plants, priced from §5 for Wildflowers to §300 for an Apple Tree. The following types of vegetation are included:

Plant Types

- **Flowers (4)**
- **Bushes (1)**
- **Hedges (2)**
- **Shrubs (2)**
- **Trees (5)**

Let your green thumb go wild, but don't forget that only trees and shrubs will thrive without regular watering. If you want colorful flowers, you'll probably need to hire a Gardener.

Fig. 5-14. This colorful landscaping will require the services of a Gardener, or a Sim with a lot of time to kill.

Special Editing Tools

In addition to the building tools described above, there are two other options on the Build Mode Control Panel. The curved arrows pictured at the bottom corner of figure 5-15 allow you to undo or repeat your last action(s). This is a quick way to delete unwanted items.

Fig. 5-15. Click Undo Last to reverse your most recent actions.

If the undo button is unavailable, you can click on the Hand Tool, select any object, and then press the Delete key to sell it back. For directions on how to delete walls, wall coverings, and floor coverings, see the appropriate sections in this chapter.

Fig. 5-16. Select an item with the Hand Tool, then press Delete to make it go away.

CHAPTER 6:
MATERIAL SIMS

Introduction

This chapter covers the eight categories of objects available in Buy Mode: Seating, Surfaces, Decorative, Electronics, Appliances, Plumbing, Lighting, and Miscellaneous. Every object is listed with its purchase price, related Motives, and Efficiency ratings. You can shop 'til you drop, but it's more important to buy smart than to buy often. Our comprehensive Buying Guide is just ahead, but first let's study some important factors that impact your spending habits.

Buying for Needs, Instead of Needing to Buy

If you select a ready-made house for your new Sim family, you acquire walls, floors, and a roof, but little else. The house is empty, with nary a toilet, bed, or refrigerator in sight. Depending upon how much you spent on the house, you'll have a few thousand Simoleans to use in Buy Mode, where you can purchase more than 150 objects. Most objects affect your Sims' environment in positive ways. However, not every object is a necessity. In fact, if you are a recovering shopping channel addict, this is not a good time to fall off your wallet. Make your first purchases with The Sims' Motives (or Needs) in mind. You can review your Sims' current Needs state by clicking on the Mood icon. We provide detailed descriptions in the Motives chapter, but for now, here is a basic shopping list that will help you get your Sims' Need bars out of the red zone during the early stages of a game.

TIP

In most instances, an expensive item has a greater impact on the related Need bar than an economy model. For example, a §300 cot gives your Sim a place to crash, but a §3,000 Mission Bed provides more Comfort and lets your Sim get by on less sleep. As an added bonus, the top-of-the-line bed also adds to the overall Room score.

Fig. 6-1. Despite logging only five hours of sleep, Bella is feeling pretty good, thanks to her §3000 Mission bed.

Fig. 6-2. A big-screen TV is fun for your Sims, but also for the neighbors, who will often hang out, and boost your Social score.

NEED	ITEM	EXPLANATION
Hunger	Refrigerator, Food Processor, Stove	A refrigerator alone will sustain life, but you will greatly improve the quality of Sim meals by using a food processor and stove. However, there is a risk of fire if your Sim doesn't have at least two Cooking Skill points.
Comfort	Bed, Chairs	Sims will sleep anywhere when they are tired, but a bed is highly recommended for sleeping, and you'll need chairs (for eating and working at the computer), and a couch for napping. A bathtub provides a little extra comfort for your Sims, but it isn't critical, provided you have a shower.
Hygiene	Sink, Shower	Dirty Sims spend a lot of time waving their arms in the air to disperse their body odor. Not a pretty sight. Fortunately, a sink and shower go a long way toward improving their state of mind (not to mention the smell).
Bladder	Toilet	When you gotta go, you gotta go. Sims prefer using a toilet, but if one is not available, they will relieve themselves on the floor. This not only causes great shame and embarrassment, but someone in your family will have to clean up the mess. It's also very bad for your Hygiene levels.
Energy	Bed	If you don't want to spawn a family of insomniacs, buy a sufficient number of beds for your Sims. A shot of coffee or espresso provides a temporary Energy boost, but it is definitely not a long-term solution.
Fun	TV	The boob tube is the easiest and cheapest way to give your Sims a break from their daily grinds. You can add other, more exciting, items later, but this is your best choice early on.
Social	Telephone	Ignore this for a short time while you focus on setting up your house. However, don't force your Sims into a solitary lifestyle. Other Sims may walk by the house, but you'll have better results after buying a telephone, so that you can invite people over and gain Social points when they arrive.
Room	Windows, Lamps, Decorations, Landscaping	Sims like plenty of light, from windows during the day and artificial lighting at night. Table Lamps are the cheapest, but they can only be placed on raised surfaces. As your game progresses, you can add decorations and landscaping to boost the Room score.

Sims Can Be Hard to Please

Given a fat bank account, it would seem that you can always cheer up your Sims with a few expensive purchases. Not exactly. While you are spending your hard-earned Simoleans, the Sims are busy comparing everything that you buy to everything they already own. If you fail to keep your Sims in the manner to which they are accustomed, their responses to your new objects may be indifferent or even downright negative. Every time you make a purchase, the game uses an assessment formula to calculate your Sim's response. The logic goes like this:

Fig. 6-3. Compared to the §2,100 "Snails With Icicles in Nose," this §45 clown picture doesn't quite stack up.

Your Diminishing Net Worth

When times are tough, you may need to raise cash by selling objects in your house. With rare exception, you will never match your initial investment, thanks to instant depreciation, and as time goes on, your belongings continue to lose value until they reach their depreciation limits. The following table lists every object in *The Sims* (alphabetically), including purchase price and depreciated values.

- **Calculates the average value of everything in your house (including outdoor items).**

- **Subtracts 10 percent of the new object's value for each existing copy of the same item. Don't expect your family members to jump for joy if you add a hot tub to every room in the house.**

- **Compares the value of the new object with all existing objects in your house. If the new purchase is worth 20 percent or more above the average value of current items, the Sim exhibits a positive response by clapping.**

- **If the new object is within 20 percent (above or below) of the current average value of all items in your household, the Sim gives you an uninspired shrug.**

- **If the new object is less than 20 percent below the average value, your Sim waves it off and you'll see a red X through the object.**

Although depreciation reduces the value of your furnishings over time, there is a buyer's remorse period when you can return the item for full value (if it has been less than 24 hours since you purchased it). So, if you have second thoughts about that new hot tub, simply select the item and hit the Delete key to get your money back.

Fig. 6-4. This Pyrotorre Gas Range is §1,000 new, but after depreciation it's worth only §790.

Object Depreciation

NAME	PURCHASE PRICE	INITIAL DEPRECIATION	DAILY DEPRECIATION	DEPRECIATION LIMIT
Alarm: Burglar	§250	§62	§2	§50
Alarm: Smoke	§50	§12	§0	§10
Aquarium	§200	§30	§2	§80
Bar	§800	§120	§8	§320
Barbecue	§350	§70	§4	§105
Basketball Hoop (Cheap Eaze)	§650	§98	§6	§260
Bed: Double	§450	§68	§4	§180
Bed: Double (Mission)	§3,000	§450	§30	§1,200
Bed: Double (Napoleon)	§1,000	§150	§10	§400
Bed: Single (Spartan)	§300	§45	§3	§120
Bed: Single (Tyke Nyte)	§450	§68	§4	§180
Bench: Garden	§250	§38	§2	§100
Bookshelf: Amishim	§500	§75	§5	§200
Bookshelf: Libri di Regina	§900	§135	§9	§360
Bookshelf: Pine	§250	§38	§2	§100
Chair: Deck (Survivall)	§150	§22	§2	§60
Chair: Dining (Empress)	§600	§90	§6	§240
Chair: Dining (Parisienne)	§1,200	§180	§12	§480
Chair: Dining (Teak)	§200	§30	§2	§80
Chair: Dining (Werkbunnst)	§80	§12	§1	§32
Chair: Living Room (Citronel)	§450	§68	§4	§180
Chair: Living Room (Country Class)	§250	§38	§2	§100
Chair: Living Room (Sarrbach)	§500	§75	§5	§200
Chair: Living Room (Wicker)	§80	§12	§1	§32
Chair: Office	§100	§15	§1	§40

NAME	PURCHASE PRICE	INITIAL DEPRECIATION	DAILY DEPRECIATION	DEPRECIATION LIMIT
Chair: Recliner (Back Slack)	§250	§38	§2	§100
Chair: Recliner (Von Braun)	§850	§128	§8	§340
Chess Set	§500	§75	§5	§200
Clock: Alarm	§30	§4	§0	§12
Clock: Grandfather	§3,500	§525	§35	§1,400
Coffee: Espresso Machine	§450	§90	§4	§135
Coffeemaker	§85	§17	§1	§26
Computer (Brahma 2000)	§2,800	§700	§28	§560
Computer (Marco)	§6,500	§1,625	§65	§1,300
Computer (Microscotch)	§1,800	§450	§18	§360
Computer (Moneywell)	§999	§250	§10	§200
Counter: Bath (Count Blanc)	§400	§60	§4	§160
Counter: Kitchen (Barcelona: In)	§800	§120	§8	§320
Counter: Kitchen (Barcelona: Out)	§800	§120	§8	§320
Counter: Kitchen (NuMica)	§150	§22	§2	§60
Counter: Kitchen (Tiled)	§250	§38	§2	§100
Desk (Cupertino)	§220	§33	§2	§88
Desk (Mesquite)	§80	§12	§1	§32
Desk (Redmond)	§800	§120	§8	§320
Dishwasher (Dish Duster)	§550	§110	§6	§165
Dishwasher (Fuzzy Logic)	§950	§190	§10	§285
Dollhouse	§180	§27	§2	§72
Dresser (Antique Armoire)	§1,200	§180	§12	§480
Dresser (Kinderstuff)	§300	§45	§3	§120

NAME	PURCHASE PRICE	INITIAL DEPRECIATION	DAILY DEPRECIATION	DEPRECIATION LIMIT
Dresser (Oak Armoire)	§550	§82	§6	§220
Dresser (Pinegulcher)	§250	§38	§2	§100
Easel	§250	§38	§2	§100
Exercise Machine	§700	§105	§7	§280
Flamingo	§12	§2	§0	§5
Food Processor	§220	§44	§2	§66
Fountain	§700	§105	§7	§280
Fridge (Freeze Secret)	§2,500	§500	§25	§750
Fridge (Llamark)	§600	§120	§6	§180
Fridge (Porcina)	§1,200	§240	§12	§360
Hot Tub	§6,500	§1,300	§65	§1,950
Lamp: Floor (Halogen)	§50	§8	§0	§20
Lamp: Floor (Lumpen)	§100	§15	§1	§40
Lamp: Floor (Torchosteronne)	§350	§52	§4	§140
Lamp: Garden	§50	§7	§1	§20
Lamp: Love n' Haight Lava	§80	§12	§1	§32
Lamp: Table (Antique)	§300	§45	§3	§120
Lamp: Table (Bottle)	§25	§4	§0	§10
Lamp: Table (Ceramiche)	§85	§13	§1	§34
Lamp: Table (Elite)	§180	§27	§2	§72
Medicine Cabinet	§125	§19	§1	§50
Microwave	§250	§50	§2	§75
Mirror: Floor	§150	§22	§2	§60
Mirror: Wall	§100	§15	§1	§40
Phone: Tabletop	§50	§12	§0	§10
Phone: Wall	§75	§19	§1	§15
Piano	§3,500	§525	§35	§1,400
Pinball Machine	§1,800	§450	§18	§360
Plant: Big (Cactus)	§150	§22	§2	§60
Plant: Big (Jade)	§160	§24	§2	§64
Plant: Big (Rubber)	§120	§18	§1	§48

NAME	PURCHASE PRICE	INITIAL DEPRECIATION	DAILY DEPRECIATION	DEPRECIATION LIMIT
Plant: Small (Geranium)	§45	§7	§0	§18
Plant: Small (Spider)	§35	§5	§0	§14
Plant: Small (Violets)	§30	§4	§0	§12
Play Structure	§1,200	§180	§12	§480
Pool Table	§4,200	§630	§42	§1,680
Shower	§650	§130	§6	§195
Sink: Bathroom Pedestal	§400	§80	§4	§120
Sink: Kitchen (Double)	§500	§100	§5	§150
Sink: Kitchen (Single)	§250	§50	§2	§75
Sofa (Blue Pinstripe)	§400	§60	§4	§160
Sofa (Contempto)	§200	§30	§2	§80
Sofa (Country)	§450	§68	§4	§180
Sofa (Deiter)	§1,100	§165	§11	§440
Sofa (Dolce)	§1,450	§218	§14	§580
Sofa (Recycled)	§180	§27	§2	§72
Sofa (SimSafari)	§220	§33	§2	§88
Sofa: Loveseat (Blue Pinstripe)	§360	§54	§4	§144
Sofa: Loveseat (Contempto)	§150	§22	§2	§60
Sofa: Loveseat (Country)	§340	§51	§3	§136
Sofa: Loveseat (Indoor-Outdoor)	§160	§24	§2	§64
Sofa: Loveseat (Luxuriare)	§875	§131	§9	§350
Stereo (Strings)	§2,550	§638	§26	§510
Stereo (Zimantz)	§650	§162	§6	§130
Stereo: Boom Box	§100	§25	§1	§20
Stove (Dialectric)	§400	§80	§4	§120
Stove (Pyrotorre)	§1,000	§200	§10	§300
Table: Dining (Colonial)	§200	§30	§2	§80
Table: Dining (Mesa)	§450	§68	§4	§180

NAME	PURCHASE PRICE	INITIAL DEPRECIATION	DAILY DEPRECIATION	DEPRECIATION LIMIT
Table: Dining (NuMica)	§95	§14	§1	§38
Table: Dining (Parisienne)	§1,200	§180	§12	§480
Table: End (Anywhere)	§120	§18	§1	§48
Table: End (Imperious)	§135	§20	§1	§54
Table: End (KinderStuff)	§75	§11	§1	§30
Table: End (Mission)	§250	§38	§2	§100
Table: End (Pinegulcher)	§40	§6	§0	§16
Table: End (Sumpto)	§300	§45	§3	§120
Table: End (Wicker)	§55	§8	§1	§22
Table: Outdoor (Backwoods)	§200	§30	§2	§80
Toaster Oven	§100	§20	§1	§30
Toilet (Flush Force)	§1,200	§240	§12	§360
Toilet (Hygeia-O-Matic)	§300	§60	§3	§90
Tombstone/Urn	§5	§1	§0	§2
Toy Box	§50	§8	§0	§20
Train Set: Large	§955	§239	§10	§191
Train Set: Small	§80	§20	§1	§16
Trash Compactor	§375	§75	§4	§112
Tub (Hydrothera)	§3,200	§640	§32	§960
Tub (Justa)	§800	§160	§8	§240
Tub (Sani-Queen)	§1,500	§300	§15	§450
TV (Monochrome)	§85	§21	§1	§17
TV (Soma)	§3,500	§875	§35	§700
TV (Trottco)	§500	§125	§5	§100
VR Glasses	§2,300	§575	§23	§460

The Sims Buying Guide

The following sections represent the eight item categories that appear when you click the Buy Mode button on the control panel. We've added a few subcategories to make it easier to find a specific object. The Efficiency Value (1–10) indicates how well the item satisfies each Motive. You get what you pay for in *The Sims*, so an §80 chair doesn't quite stack up to an §850 recliner when it comes to boosting your Comfort level, and it cannot restore Energy.

Seating

Chairs

There are three types of chairs in *The Sims*: movable, stationary, and reclining. Any chair will function at a desk or table for eating and using objects. If your budget is tight, you can also use cheaper chairs for watching TV or reading, but their Comfort ratings are very low. You can use high-ticket dining room chairs at the computer, but that is probably overkill. You are better off placing them in the dining room where you receive greater benefit from their enhanced Room ratings.

Stationary chairs are cushier and nicely upholstered (depending on your taste, of course), and they usually provide more comfort. Finally, the reclining chairs are top of the line, giving you increased comfort and the added benefit of being able to catch a few Zs in the reclining position.

TIP

Chair placement is critical, especially around tables. A Sim will not move a chair sideways, only forward and backward. So, position the chair properly or the Sim will not be able to use the table (or what is on it). Also, be careful not to trap a Sim in a corner when a chair is pulled out. For example, if a child is playing with a train set in the corner of the room, and another Sim pulls out a chair to use the computer, the child would be trapped in the corner until the computer user is finished.

Werkbunnst All-Purpose Chair

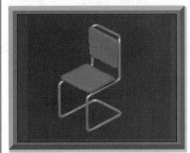

Type: Movable

Cost: §80

Motive: Comfort (2)

Posture Plus Office Chair

Type: Movable

Cost: §100

Motive: Comfort (3)

Deck Chair by Survivall

Type: Movable

Cost: §150

Motive: Comfort (3)

Parisienne Dining Chair

Type: Movable

Cost: §1,200

Motives: Comfort (6), Room (3)

Touch of Teak Dinette Chair

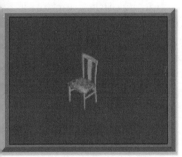

Type: Movable

Cost: §200

Motive: Comfort (3)

Sioux City Wicker Chair

Type: Stationary

Cost: §80

Motive: Comfort (2)

Empress Dining Room Chair

Type: Movable

Cost: §600

Motives: Comfort (4), Room (2)

Country Class Armchair

Type: Stationary

Cost: §250

Motive: Comfort (4)

"Citronel" from Chiclettina Inc.

Type: Stationary

Cost: §450

Motive: Comfort (6)

"The Sarrbach" by Werkbunnst

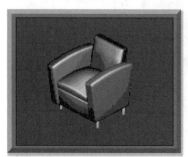

Type: Stationary

Cost: §500

Motive: Comfort (6)

"Back Slack" Recliner

Type: Recliner

Cost: §250

Motives: Comfort (6), Energy (3)

"Von Braun" Recliner

Type: Recliner

Cost: §850

Motives: Comfort (9), Energy (3)

Couches

Sitting down is fine for reading, eating, or working, but for serious vegging, your Sims need a good couch. When selecting a couch, function is more important than quality. If you are looking for a place to take naps, pay more attention to the Energy rating than the Comfort or Room ratings. A multipurpose couch should have good Energy and Comfort ratings. However, if you are furnishing your party area, select one that looks good, thereby enhancing your Room rating. Stay away from the cheapest couches (under §200). For a few extra dollars, a medium-priced couch will make your Sims a lot happier. When you're flush with Simoleans, don't forget to dress up your garden with the outdoor bench. You can't sleep on it, but it looks great.

Contempto Loveseat

Cost: §150

Motives: Comfort (3), Energy (4)

ndoor-Outdoor Loveseat

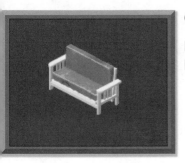

Cost: §160

Motives: Comfort (3), Energy (4)

SimSafari Sofa

Cost: §220

Motives: Comfort (3), Energy (5)

Recycled Couch

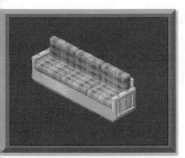

Cost: §180

Motives: Comfort (2), Energy (5)

Parque Fresco del Aire Bench

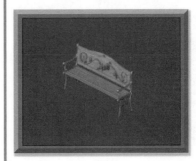

Cost: §250

Motive: Comfort (2)

Contempto Couch

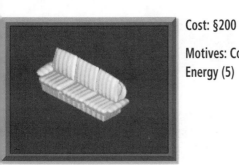

Cost: §200

Motives: Comfort (3), Energy (5)

Country Class Loveseat

Cost: §340

Motives: Comfort (5), Energy (4)

Pinstripe Loveseat from Zecutime

Cost: §360

Motives: Comfort (5), Energy (4)

Luxuriare Loveseat

Cost: §875

Motives: Comfort (8), Energy (4), Room (2)

Pinstripe Sofa from Zecutime

Cost: §400

Motives: Comfort (5), Energy (5)

"The Deiter" by Werkbunnst

Cost: §1,100

Motives: Comfort (8), Energy (5), Room (3)

Country Class Sofa

Cost: §450

Motives: Comfort (5), Energy (5)

Dolce Tutti Frutti Sofa

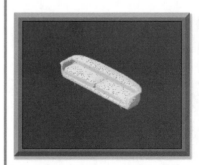

Cost: §1,450

Motives: Comfort (9), Energy (5), Room (3)

Beds

Getting enough sleep can be one of the most frustrating goals in *The Sims*, especially if there is a new baby in the house, or your car pool arrives at some ungodly hour of the morning. In the early stages of a game, it is not important to spend a bundle of money on a designer bed. However, an upgrade later on is well worth the money, because a top-of-the-line bed recharges your Energy bar faster.

Tyke Nyte Bed

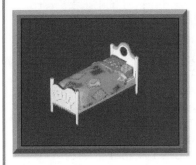

Cost: §450

Motives: Comfort (7), Energy (7)

Spartan Special

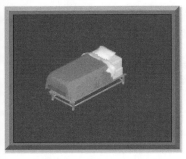

Cost: §300

Motives: Comfort (6), Energy (7)

Napoleon Sleigh Bed

Cost: §1,000

Motives: Comfort (8), Energy (9)

Cheap Eazzzzze Double Sleeper

Cost: §450

Motives: Comfort (7), Energy (8)

Modern Mission Bed

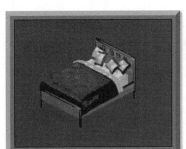

Cost: §3,000

Motives: Comfort (9), Energy (10), Room (3)

Surfaces

Sims will eat or read standing up if they have to, but they won't be particularly happy about it. Sitting at a table while eating a meal bolsters a Sim's Comfort. Since your Sims have to eat to satisfy Hunger, they might as well improve Comfort, too. Many objects require elevated surfaces, so allow enough room for nightstands (alarm clock, lamps), tables (computer), and countertops (microwave, coffeemaker, etc.), when you design the interior of your house. Also, your Sims cannot prepare food on a table, so provide ample countertop space in the kitchen, or you may find them wandering into the bathroom to chop veggies on the counter (hair in the soup—yummy!).

Countertops

NuMica Kitchen Counter

Cost: §150

Motive: None

Tiled Counter

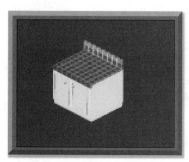

Cost: §250

Motive: None

Count Blanc Bathroom Counter

Cost: §400

Motive: None

"Barcelona" Outcurve Counter

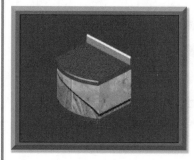

Cost: §800

Motive: Room (2)

"Barcelona" Incurve Counter

Cost: §800

Motive: Room (2)

End Tables

Pinegulcher End Table

Cost: §40

Motive: None

Wicker Breeze End Table

Cost: §55

Motive: None

"Anywhere" End Table

Cost: §120

Motive: None

Imperious Island End Table

Cost: §135

Motive: None

Modern Mission End Table

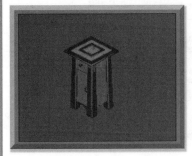

Cost: §250

Motive: Room (1)

Sumpto End Table

Cost: §300

Motive: Room (1)

KinderStuff Nightstand

Cost: §75

Motive: None

Desks/Tables

Mesquite Desk/Table

Cost: §80

Motive: None

NuMica Folding Card Table

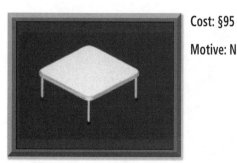

Cost: §95

Motive: None

"Colonial Legacy" Dining Table

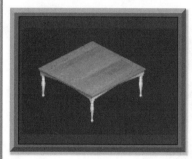

Cost: §200

Motive: None

Backwoods Table by Survivall

Cost: §200

Motive: None

London "Cupertino" Collection Desk/Table

Cost: §220

Motive: None

London "Mesa" Dining Design

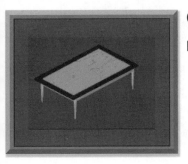

Cost: §450

Motive: Room (2)

The "Redmond" Desk/Table

Cost: §800

Motive: Room (2)

Parisienne Dining Table

Cost: §1,200

Motive: Room (3)

Decorative

After the essential furnishings are in place, you can improve your Room score by adding decorative objects. Some items, such as the grandfather clock and aquarium, require regular maintenance, but most decorative items exist solely for your Sims' viewing pleasure. You might even get lucky and buy a painting or sculpture that increases in value. In addition to enhancing the Room score, the aquarium and fountain have Fun value.

Pink Flamingo

Cost: §12

Motive: Room (2)

African Violet

Cost: §30

Motive: Room (1)

Spider Plant

Cost: §35

Motive: Room (1)

Watercolor by J.M.E.

Cost: §75

Motive: Room (1)

"Roxana" Geranium

Cost: §45

Motive: Room (1)

Rubber Tree Plant

Cost: §120

Motive: Room (2)

"Tragic Clown" Painting

Cost: §45

Motive: Room (1)

Echinopsis maximus Cactus

Cost: §150

Motive: Room (2)

Jade Plant

Cost: §160

Motive: Room (2)

"Delusion de Grandeur"

Cost: §360

Motive: Room (2)

Poseidon's Adventure Aquarium

Cost: §200

Motive: Fun (1), Room (2)

"Fountain of Tranquility"

Cost: §700

Motives: Fun (1), Room (2)

"Bi-Polar" by Conner I.N.

Cost: §240

Motive: Room (2)

Landscape #12,001 by Manny Kopees

Cost: §750

Motive: Room (3)

Bust of Athena by Klassick Repro. Inc.

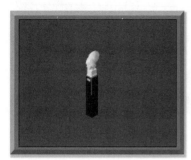

Cost: §875

Motive: Room (3)

"Scylla and Charybdis"

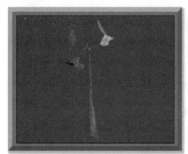

Cost: §1,450

Motive: Room (4)

Snails With Icicles in Nose

Cost: §2,140

Motive: Room (5)

Portrait Grid by Payne A. Pitcher

Cost: §3,200

Motive: Room (8)

Grandfather Clock

Cost: §3,500

Motive: Room (7)

Blue China Vase

Cost: §4,260

Motive: Room (7)

"Still Life, Drapery and Crumbs"

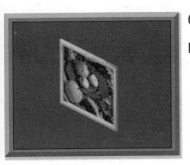

Cost: §7,600

Motive: Room (9)

"Large Black Slab" by ChiChi Smith

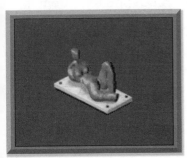

Cost: §12,648

Motive: Room (10)

Electronics

This game offers a veritable potpourri of high-tech gadgetry, ranging from potentially lifesaving items such as smoke detectors to nonessential purchases such as pinball games or virtual reality headsets. Beyond the critical electronics items—smoke detectors, telephone for receiving calls or calling services and friends, TV for cheap fun, and computer for finding a job—you should focus on items with group activity potential, especially if you like socializing and throwing parties.

Electronic items can break down on a regular basis, so it is a good idea to bone up on Mechanical Skills. Until you have a qualified fix-it Sim in the house, you'll be shelling out §50 an hour for a repairman.

FireBrand Smoke Detector

Cost: §50

Motive: None

Notes: Each detector covers one room. At the very least, place a detector in any room that has a stove or fireplace.

SimSafety IV Burglar Alarm

Cost: §250

Motive: None

Notes: An alarm unit covers one room, but an outside alarm covers an area within five tiles of the house. The police are called immediately when the alarm goes off.

SCTC BR-8 Standard Telephone

Cost: §50

Motive: None

Notes: This phone needs a surface, so it's less accessible. Best location is in the kitchen; stick with wall phones in the rest of the house.

SCTC Cordless Wall Phone

Cost: §75

Motive: None

Notes: Place these phones wherever your Sims spend a lot of time.

Urchineer Train Set by Rip Co.

Cost: §80

Motive: Fun (2)

Notes: Group activity; can only be used by kids.

Televisions

Buying a TV is the easiest way to put a little fun into your Sims' lives, and it is a group activity. You can maximize the effect by matching the program category with your Sim's personality, as noted in the following table.

PERSONALITY	FAVORITE TV SHOW
Active	Action
Grouchy (low nice)	Horror
Outgoing	Romance
Playful	Cartoon

Your TV will eventually break down, especially if you have a family of couch potatoes. Do not attempt to repair the TV unless your Sim has at least one Mechanical Skill point (three is even better). If your Sim doesn't have the proper training, poking around inside the TV will result in electrocution.

Monochrome TV

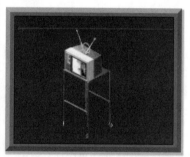

Cost: §85

Motive: Fun (2)

Notes: Strictly for tight budgets, but it gives your Sims a little mindless fun.

Trottco 27" Color Television B94U

Cost: §500

Motive: Fun (4)

Notes: A lazy Sim's favorite activity is watching TV.

Soma Plasma TV

Cost: §3,500

Motive: Fun (6), Room (2)

Notes: It's expensive, but it provides instant entertainment for a full house.

Stereos

Dancing to the music is a great group activity, especially for Sims with effervescent personalities (although it is perfectly acceptable to dance alone). When a Sim dances with a houseguest, it increases both their Fun and Social ratings. You can personalize *The Sims* by placing your own MP3 files in the Music/Stations directory.

"Down Wit Dat" Boom Box

Cost: §100

Motive: Fun (2)

Notes: An inexpensive way to start a party in your front yard.

Zimantz Component Hi-Fi Stereo

Cost: §650

Motive: Fun (3)

Notes: Perfect for your big party room.

Strings Theory Stereo

Cost: §2,550

Motives: Fun (5), Room (3)

Notes: The ultimate party machine, this is the only stereo that enhances your Room score.

Computers

A computer is a Sim's best tool for finding a job. The computer has three job postings every day, making it three times as productive as the newspaper employment ads. Aside from career search, the computer provides entertainment for the entire family, and it helps the kids keep their grades up (better chance of cash rewards from the grandparents). Playful and lazy Sims love the computer. However, if only serious Sims occupy your house, you can grab a newspaper and let the age of technology pass you by.

Moneywell Computer

Cost: §999

Motive: Fun (3), Study

Notes: All you need is a basic computer for job searching.

Microscotch Covetta Q628-1500JA

Cost: §1,800

Motive: Fun (5), Study

Notes: More power translates into better gaming.

The Brahma 2000

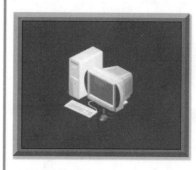

Cost: §2,800

Motive: Fun (7), Study

Notes: More than twice the fun of a basic computer.

Meet Marco

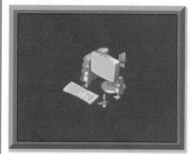

Cost: §6,500

Motive: Fun (9), Study

Notes: For Sim power users—the family will fight for playing time on this beast.

OCD Systems SimRailRoad Town

Cost: §955

Motive: Fun (4), Room (3)

Notes: You need a large area for this train table, but it is an excellent group activity and it gives a serious boost to your Room score.

"See Me, Feel Me" Pinball Machine

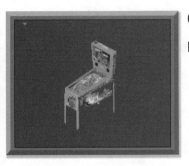

Cost: §1,800

Motive: Fun (5)

Notes: Build a big family room and add a pinball machine to keep your guests occupied for hours.

SSRI Virtual Reality Set

Cost: §2,300

Motive: Fun (7)

Notes: Playful Sims have been known to don VR glasses on their way to the bathroom (even with full bladders). For grins, wait until a Sim puts on the glasses, then immediately issue another command. The Sim head on the control panel will wear the glasses for the duration of your game.

Appliances

With the exception of the dishwasher and trash compactor, the Sim appliances are all devoted to the creation of food or java. At a bare minimum, you need refrigeration. However, if you want your Sims to eat like royalty, train at least one family member in the gentle art of cooking and provide that Sim with the latest in culinary tools.

Mr. Regular-Joe Coffee

Cost: §85

Motive: Bladder (-1), Energy (1)

Notes: Only adults can partake of the coffee rush. The effects are temporary, but sometimes it's the only way to get rolling.

Gagmia Simore Espresso Machine

Cost: §450

Motive: Bladder (-2), Energy (2), Fun (1)

Notes: If you want a morning jolt, espresso is the way to go. You'll fill your bladder twice as fast as with regular coffee, but it is a small price to pay for more energy and a splash of fun.

Brand Name Toaster Oven

Cost: §100

Motive: Hunger (1)

Notes: This little roaster is better at starting fires than cooking food. Improve your Cooking Skills and buy a real oven. Until then, use a microwave.

Positive Potential Microwave

Cost: §250

Motive: Hunger (2)

Notes: You can warm up your food without burning the house down.

Dialectric Free Standing Range

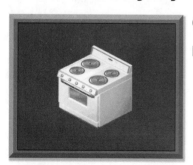

Cost: §400

Motive: Hunger (5)

Notes: After raising your Cooking Skills to three or above, you can create nutritious (and satisfying) meals on this stove.

The "Pyrotorre" Gas Range

Cost: §1,000

Motive: Hunger (7)

Notes: A skilled chef can create works of art on this stove.

NOTE

Although an expensive stove enhances your Sim meals, it is only one of three steps in the cooking process. To maximize the potential of your stove, you need an excellent refrigerator for storage, and a food processor for efficient preparation.

Wild Bill THX-451 Barbecue

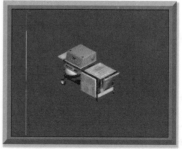

Cost: §350

Motive: Hunger (4)

Notes: Only experienced adult chefs should fire up the barbecue. Be careful not to position the grill near flammable items.

XLR8R Food Processor

Cost: §220

Motive: Hunger (2)

Notes: A food processor speeds up meal preparation and enhances food quality.

Junk Genie Trash Compactor

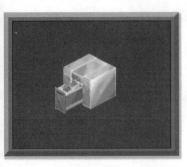

Cost: §375

Motive: None

Notes: A compactor holds more garbage than a trash can, and even when it is full, it will not degrade the Room rating because the trash is concealed.

Dish Duster Deluxe

Cost: §550

Motive: Dirty dishes lower your Room score.

Notes: Kids can't use the dishwasher, but it still cuts cleanup time considerably, and the countertop can be used for placing other items (sorry, no eating allowed).

Fuzzy Logic Dishwasher

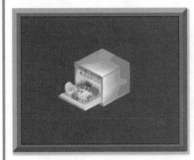

Cost: §950

Motive: Dirty dishes lower your Room score.

Notes: The Cadillac of dishwashers cleans up kitchen messes in a snap. This model has fewer breakdowns than the Dish Duster.

Llamark Refrigerator

Cost: §600

Motive: Hunger (6)

Notes: This model is sufficient while your Sims are building up their Cooking Skills.

Porcina Refrigerator Model P1g-S

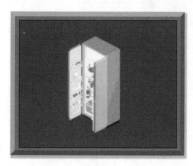

Cost: §1,200

Motive: Hunger (7)

Notes: This model produces more satisfying food for your Sims.

Freeze Secret Refrigerator

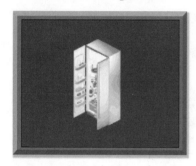

Cost: §2,500

Motive: Hunger (8)

Notes: The best place to store your food. When it's matched with a food processor, gas stove, and an experienced chef, your Sims will be licking their lips.

Plumbing

Sims can't carry buckets to the well for their weekly bath, and the outhouse hasn't worked in years, so install various plumbing objects to maintain a clean, healthy environment. Of course, not every plumbing object is essential, but you can't beat a relaxing hour in the hot tub with a few of your closest friends (or casual acquaintances).

Hydronomic Kitchen Sink

Cost: §250

Motive: Hygiene (2)

Notes: Without it the Sims would be washing dishes in the bathroom.

Epikouros Kitchen Sink

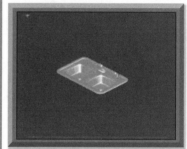

Cost: §500

Motive: Hygiene (3)

Notes: It's twice as big as the single, but a dishwasher is a better investment.

"Andersonville" Pedestal Sink

Cost: §400

Motive: Hygiene (2)

Notes: Neat Sims like to wash their hands after using the toilet.

Hygeia-O-Matic Toilet

Cost: §300

Motive: Bladder (8)

Notes: Hey, your only other option is the floor.

Flush Force 5 XLT

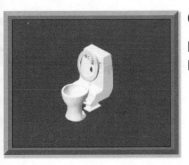

Cost: §1,200

Motives: Comfort (4), Bladder (8)

Notes: Your Sims can't go to the ballpark to get a good seat, but they can sit in a lap of luxury in the bathroom.

SpaceMiser Shower

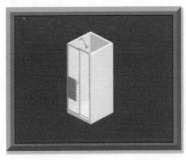

Cost: §650

Motive: Hygiene (6)

Notes: This is basic equipment in a Sims bathroom. One Sim can shower at a time, and the neat ones tend to linger longer than the sloppy ones. Sims are generally shy if they are not in love with a housemate, so you may need more than one shower (and bathroom) to prevent a traffic jam in the bathroom.

Justa Bathtub

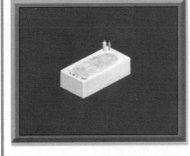

Cost: §800

Motives: Comfort (3), Hygiene (6)

Notes: Your Sims get a double benefit from a relaxing bath when they have a little extra time.

Sani-Queen Bathtub

Cost: §1,500

Motives: Comfort (5), Hygiene (8)

Notes: Almost twice the price, but the added Comfort and Hygiene points are worth it.

Hydrothera Bathtub

Cost: §3,200

Motives: Comfort (8), Hygiene (10)

Notes: The most fun a Sim can have alone. Save your Simoleans, buy it, and listen to sounds of relaxation.

WhirlWizard Hot Tub

Cost: §6,500

Motives: Comfort (6), Hygiene (2), Fun (2)

Notes: Up to four adult Sims can relax, mingle, and begin lasting relationships in the hot tub.

Lighting

Sims love natural light, so make sure the sun shines through your windows from every direction. And, when the sun goes down, your Sims need plenty of lighting on the walls, floors, and tables to illuminate their world until bedtime. Although only three lamps listed below have direct impact on the Room score, all of the lamps have a collective effect when spread evenly throughout the home. Pay special attention to key activity areas in the kitchen, family room, bedrooms, and of course, the bathroom.

CAUTION

Lamp bulbs burn out with use, and they must be replaced. Sims can replace their own bulbs, but without Mechanical Skills, they run the risk of electrocution. Hiring a repairman is another option, but at §50 per hour, this can be very costly.

Table Lamps

Bottle Lamp

Cost: §25

Motive: None

Love n' Haight Lava Lamp

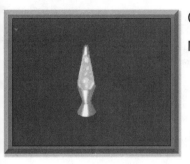

Cost: §80

Motive: Room (2)

Ceramiche Table Lamp

Cost: §85

Motive: None

Elite Reflections Chrome Lamp

Cost: §180

Motive: None

SC Electric Co. Antique Lamp

Cost: §300

Motive: Room (1)

Floor Lamps

Halogen Heaven Lamp by Contempto

Cost: §50

Motive: None

Lumpen Lumeniat Floor Lamp

Cost: §100

Motive: None

Torchosteronne Floor Lamp

Cost: §350

Motive: Room (1)

Top Brass Sconce

Cost: §110

Motive: None

Wall Lamps

White Globe Sconce

Cost: §35

Motive: None

Blue Plate Special Sconce

Cost: §135

Motive: None

Oval Glass Sconce

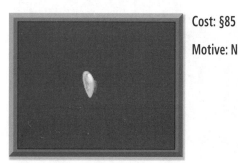

Cost: §85

Motive: None

Outside Lamp

Garden Lamp (Outdoor Use Only)

Cost: §50

Motive: None

Miscellaneous

We're down to the objects that are hard to fit into a category—everything from bookcases to beverage bars. Don't make the mistake of ignoring these items because you think they're luxuries; your Sim's life would be extremely difficult without a trash can, alarm clock, and bookcase. Plus, if you want to improve your Sim's Charisma and Body ratings, you'll need a mirror and exercise machine. So, once you install the basic objects in your house, look to the Miscellaneous category for objects that take your Sim's lifestyle to the next level.

SnoozMore Alarm Clock

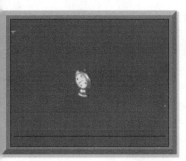

Cost: §30

Motive: None

Notes: After you set the clock, it will ring two hours before the carpool arrives for every working Sim in your house.

Trash Can

Cost: §30

Motive: None

Notes: Without a place to put trash, your Sim house will become a fly-infested hovel.

Magical Mystery Toy Box

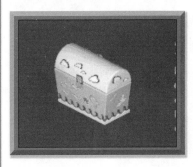

Cost: §50

Motive: Fun (2)

Notes: A good entertainment alternative if your kids are getting bleary-eyed in front of the computer.

Narcisco Wall Mirror

Cost: §100

Motive: Improves Charisma

Notes: Adults can Practice speech in front of the mirror to improve their Charisma.

Medicine Cabinet

Cost: §125

Motive: Hygiene (1), Improves Charisma

Notes: Your Sims can Practice speech in the bathroom and improve their Hygiene at the same time.

Narcisco Floor Mirror

Cost: §150

Motive: Improves Charisma

Notes: Place this mirror anywhere to practice Charisma without locking other Sims out of the bathroom.

Will Lloyd Wright Doll House

Cost: §180

Motive: Fun (2)

Notes: An engaging group activity for kids and adults.

Cheap Pine Bookcase

Cost: §250

Motive: Fun (1), Improve Cooking, Mechanical, and Study Skills

Notes: Reading books is the best way to prevent premature death from fires or electrocution.

"Dimanche" Folding Easel

Cost: §250

Motive: Fun (2), Improves Creativity

Notes: With practice, a Sim can improve Creativity, and eventually sell a picture for up to §166.

Pinegulcher Dresser

Cost: §250

Motive: None

Notes: A Sim can change into various formal, work, and leisure outfits, and even acquire a new body type.

Kinderstuff Dresser

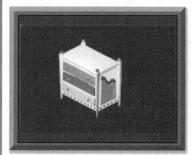

Cost: §300

Motive: None

Notes: Kids like to dress up too!

Amishim Bookcase

Cost: §500

Motive: Fun (2), Improves Cooking, Mechanical, and Study Skills

Notes: This expensive bookcase awards Skill points at the same rate as the cheaper one.

Chuck Matewell Chess Set

Cost: §500

Motive: Fun (2), Improves Logic

Notes: Serious Sims gain the most Fun points by playing, and any two Sims can improve Logic by playing each other.

Traditional Oak Armoire

Cost: §550

Motive: Room (1)

Notes: This dresser allows your Sim to change clothes (body skins). The choices vary, depending upon the Sim's current outfit.

SuperDoop Basketball Hoop

Cost: §650

Motive: Fun (4)

Notes: Active Sims love to play hoops, and any visitor is welcome to join the fun. A Sim with higher Body points performs better on the court.

"Exerto" Benchpress Exercise Machine

Cost: §700

Motive: Improves Body

Notes: Adult Sims can bulk up their Body points with exercise sessions.

Bachman Wood Beverage Bar

Cost: §800

Motive: Hunger (1), Fun (3), Room (2)

Notes: Every drink lowers the Bladder score, but adult Sims like to make drinks for themselves and friends. Kids can grab a soda from the fridge.

Libri di Regina Bookcase

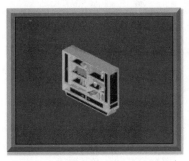

Cost: §900

Motive: Fun (3), Improves Cooking, Mechanical, and Study Skills

Notes: This stylish bookcase is perfect for a swanky Sim pad, but it still imparts Skill points at the same rate as the pine model.

Antique Armoire

Cost: §1,200

Motive: Room (2)

Notes: A more expensive version of the cheaper armoire, but it adds twice as many Room points.

The Funinator Deluxe

Cost: §1,200

Motive: Fun (5)

Notes: When the house is swarming with kids, send them outside to raise their Fun bar and burn some energy.

Chimeway & Daughters Piano

Cost: §3,500

Motive: Fun (4), Room (3), Improves Creativity

Notes: The most creative Sims will produce more beautiful music. The better the music, the greater the chance that listeners will like it. If a listener does not like the music, both Sims' Relationship scores will deteriorate.

Aristoscratch Pool Table

Cost: §4,200

Motive: Fun (6)

Notes: Up to two Sims use the table at the same time. Make sure that you allow enough room for Sims to get to the table and walk around it during play.

CHAPTER 7:
ALL IN THE FAMILY

Introduction

Up to this point, we've covered the mechanics of *The Sims*. By now you should be familiar with creating families, building houses, buying objects, and getting jobs; and you should have considerable insight into how a Sim thinks and acts. Now, let's put it all together and join several Sim households in action. In this chapter we introduce you to working Sims families, ranging from one-Sim homes to larger households with kids and babies. Finally, we take an in-depth look at one of the toughest challenges in *The Sims*: building positive (and long-lasting) Relationships.

You Can Make It Alone

The biggest difficulty in being a bachelor is that you have to do everything yourself (sounds like real life, doesn't it?). You'll need to cook, clean, and improve your Skills, while at the same time keep up with a work schedule and satisfy your personal Motives. There's always time for Fun, and a good sofa or easy chair will provide a measure of Comfort. However, it's impossible to socialize while at work, and you will be frustrated watching neighbors drop by during the day and then leave when no one answers the door.

The Single Sim's Career

As a lone Sim you must choose a job that has decent hours and light friendship demands. This leaves a Military career as your only option. At most levels you work a six-hour day, and you won't need a single friend for the first five levels. A promotion to Level 6 requires one friend, but that can be established after you refine your schedule.

Designing a Bachelor Pad

There are several considerations when designing and furnishing a house for one Sim. Review the following checklist before you place your first wall stake.

Fig. 7-1. It's hardly the lap of luxury, but you have everything you need to get a job, keep your sanity, and learn how to cook.

- **Keep your house small, and place the front door close to the street. This allows you to milk a few extra minutes out of every morning before meeting the car pool.**

- **The interior should include a bedroom, bathroom, and living room. Rather than add a family room, use an outside patio area for Fun objects and an exercise machine. A Military career requires an ever-increasing number of Body Skill points.**

- **Install only enough counter space to place a food processor and prepare your meals. This leaves more space for a table and chairs. Buy at least two chairs so that you can socialize with a friend while sharing a meal.**

- **Without the space or the budget to buy expensive sofas or recliners, get a top-of-the-line bed, which enables your Sim to get by on fewer hours of sleep. Buy an inexpensive nightstand for an alarm clock, and add a few wall lights to boost your Room score.**

- **You'll need a computer for your job search, but keep in mind that you can return it within 24 Sim-hours for a full refund. Find your Military job and then pack up the PC.**

- **Buy an expensive refrigerator to maximize the quality of your food, but don't bother with a stove until your Sim learns how to cook.**

- **Because of your career, there's no need to socialize until you are up for promotion to Level 6, so don't waste money on living room chairs or an expensive sofa. A cheap TV will provide enough Fun for now.**

Leaving the Single Life

Eventually you will tire of the solitary lifestyle, which, thanks to the romantic tendencies of most Sims, is not a problem. The first step is friendship. After the Relationship bar tops 70, your Sim needs to lay on the romance, with plenty of kissing and hugging. Eventually, the Propose option will appear on the menu.

Fig. 7-2. The kissin' and huggin' pays off; now it's time to pop the question.

A marriage proposal can only take place in the home of the proposer, so set the mood (you know, empty your Bladder somewhere other than on the floor, clean up yesterday's dishes, and hide those overdue bills). After accepting the proposal, your new spouse moves into your place, along with a good job (a good thing) and plenty of money (a really good thing). But, proposing does not guarantee a positive response. For example, a Sim will never accept the proposal on an empty stomach, so you might want to eat dinner first.

Fig. 7-3. "We're alone, the time is perfect, and I've got grass stains on my knee."

Fig. 7-4. "Nope, sorry, I can't marry you on an empty stomach. Besides, your current lover is hiding in the bushes."

Keep in mind that you have to create potential mates, because the game won't provide them. You might as well choose compatible personalities, and it doesn't hurt to spend some time on career development. Remember that another Sim can also propose to you in his or her house; so unless you want to change residences, hold the romantic interludes at your place.

NOTE

After marriage, your Sim will still share a bed with any other Sim with a high enough Friendship score (over 70), so don't be surprised if your Sim ends up on the couch when his buddy beats him to the sack.

Fig. 7-5. When two Sims decide to get married, they change clothes and complete the ceremony within seconds.

A three-way relationship makes it easier to have babies. Not only are there additional combinations for procreation, but you can also have one of the working adults take a night job, so there is a caregiver for the baby during the day. Even with staggered schedules, there will be at least one sleepless Sim until the baby matures, so don't get too complacent with this arrangement.

Interestingly, if your future spouse already has children, and at least one adult still resides in his or her original house, the kids stay. So, your new spouse arrives with job and bank account intact, sans kids. What a deal!

That isn't the only unusual aspect of married life in SimsVille. Marriage is not sacred here, at least not in the legal sense. A Sim can have multiple mates all living under the same roof, as pictured in figure 7-6. The interpersonal dynamics can sometimes get a little dicey, but it's workable, and the extra income is great!

Married, with Children

After your Sims promise undying love and devotion to each other (or, at least until the next promotion), it's time to have a baby. Actually, your Sims can live together for years without having children, but if they do, you'll be missing one of the *The Sims*' most vexing experiences.

Conception

The exercise of making a baby is similar to the steps taken to activate the marriage Proposal option. First, get a male and female Sim together, and then concentrate on strengthening their relationship. When both Sims are obviously enjoying each other's company, lay on the hugs and kisses. Keep smooching until you receive the option to have a baby, as pictured in figure 7-7.

Fig. 7-6. After the wedding, our Sim bride goes to bed with her former boyfriend.

Fig. 7-7. A little bundle of joy is just a click away.

If you answer yes, a bassinet appears almost instantly, amid an explosion of dandelions. The happy couple celebrates the new arrival, then they quickly go back to their daily routine. This baby thing is a snap. Well, not exactly.

Fig. 7-8. Yippee! It's a boy!

In short order, the little bundle of joy starts screaming. A Sim will eventually respond to the cries, but rather than wait, get someone to the baby immediately. Clicking on the bassinet reveals three options: Feed, Play, or Sing. When in doubt, Feed the baby, but be prepared to come right back with Play or Sing when the baby starts wailing again.

Fig. 7-9. Kids do a great job entertaining the baby during one of its frequent crying sessions.

This mayhem continues for three Sim days, during which time the household will be in an uproar. Forget about getting eight hours of beauty sleep. Designate one Sim as primary caregiver, preferably one who does not work, because the baby's cries wake any Sim in the room. The first day is nonstop crying. By the second day, the baby sleeps for a few hours at a time; take advantage of the break and send the caregiver to bed. As long as you stay responsive, the baby evolves into a runny-nosed kid, and the family can get back to normal. However, if you spend too much time in the hot tub and not enough time with the baby, a social service worker will march into your house and take the baby, as pictured in figure 7-10. You'll only receive one warning, so don't take this responsibility lightly.

Fig. 7-10. We hardly knew the little tyke!

NOTE

The bassinet appears near the spot where your Sims made the decision to have a baby. Although the Sims cannot move the bassinet, you can use the Hand Tool to move it. Pick a location that is isolated from other sleeping areas, so the disturbance is kept to a minimum.

Building and Maintaining Healthy Relationships

Gathering an ever-increasing number of friends is critical for career advancement, especially at the higher levels. It is also your Sims' only way to build up their Social scores and fend off frequent bouts of depression. In this section we outline the steps required for finding potential friends, building up positive feelings, and then maintaining healthy relationships.

Talk Is Cheap

The easiest way to make friends is often overlooked, because it is uneventful compared to other social events. However, you can almost always initiate a conversation between Sims (regardless of their Friendship scores), and keep it going for a very long time. During this benign exchange of thought balloons, you can usually nudge the Friendship score in a positive direction. When starting from 0 it takes a few encounters to get over 50 (true friendship), but once you reach this threshold, the action picks up considerably. Our newly married Sims went from a score of 64 to a marriage proposal in one evening. Although the woman eventually declined because her stomach was growling, she proposed the next day and the marriage was consummated.

Fig. 7-11. Keep talking and your Friendship score will grow.

Finding Time to Socialize

After your Sim starts working, it's difficult to find time to call other Sims and arrange meetings. Mornings are worst, although you have more options if your neighborhood has several non-working Sims. Your best bet is to start socializing right after coming home from work. Take care of personal needs first—Hygiene and Bladder—and then "Serve Dinner." Don't let a bad chef get near the stove; you can't afford to waste time putting out a fire or your guests will leave. With a counter full of food, your friends head straight for the kitchen, where you can chat over a plate of Sim-grub and then plan the rest of your evening.

Positive Social Events

After everyone is finished eating, take a little time for pleasant conversation. In the case of the female Sims pictured in figure 7-11, there is a lot of fence mending to accomplish, because one just stole the other's love interest. But, Sims are generally forgiving, and a quarrel can be mended with a few drinks, a game of pool, or a long soak in the hot tub.

Ideally, your house has an entertainment room with group activity items such as a pool table, stereo, or beverage bar. After you get everyone into the room, keep them busy with a string of activities. Even our former lovers can't resist a dance when the music starts playing, as pictured in figure 7-12.

Fig. 7-12. Our Sim guy is enjoying this dance with his former girlfriend, although his current wife will probably slap him when the music stops playing (if she can stay awake long enough).

Avoid close activities such as dancing, hugging, etc. when the current spouse or love interest is in the room. When the dance was over (figure 7-12), our Sim wife did indeed slap her new husband, causing her recently mended Relationship score with the other woman to drop from +14 to –7.

One of the most difficult aspects of entertaining in the evening is keeping the host from falling asleep on the floor. After a hard day's work, most Sims begin nodding out around 10:00 p.m. You can squeeze a little extra time out of the evening if they take a short nap after coming home from work. Be prepared for a grouchy Sim in the morning (figure 7-13) if the evening's festivities stretch too far into the night.

Fig. 7-13. Our tired party girl hurries off to the car pool without a shower—not a good way to impress her superiors.

After your guests arrive, you need to micromanage your Sims so they don't go off and take care of their own needs. Obviously, you must pay attention to a full Bladder, but you can delay other actions by redirecting your Sims to group activities. Break up the party when your Sims are teetering on the edge of exhaustion or they'll fall asleep on the floor.

Visiting Sims generally hang around until 1:00 a.m. or later, which is undoubtedly past your bedtime. Direct your Sims to bed at the appropriate time, or they may feel compelled to hang out with their guests until well past midnight, as pictured in figure 7-14.

Fig. 7-14. Our host Sim is still cleaning up dishes when he should be asleep.

Stockpiling Potential Friends

When your career advances to the top promotion level, you need more than 10 friends in every career except the Military. Hence, it's a good idea to create a few additional families early in the game, and you might want to fill one house with the maximum of eight Sims to dramatically increase your pool.

Visitors Coming and Going

The following tables include important information on how and why visitors do the things they do. You may not be able to directly control your guests' actions, but at least you won't take it personally when they decide to split.

Visitors' Starting Motives

MOTIVE	STARTING VALUE
Bladder	0 to 30
Comfort	30 to 70
Energy	35
Fun	-20 to 20
Hunger	-30 to -20
Hygiene	90
Social	-50 to -40

In a perfect Sim-world, visitors leave your house just past 1:00 a.m. However if one of their Motives falls into the danger zone, they will depart earlier. When this happens, the Sim's thought balloon reveals a reason for the early exit.

Visitors' Leaving Motives

MOTIVE	DROPS BELOW THIS VALUE
Bladder	-90
Comfort	-70
Energy	-80
Fun	-55
Hunger	-50
Hygiene	-70
Mood	-75
Room	-100
Social	-85

Guest Activities

There are three types of visitor activities: those initiated by a family member, shared activities, and autonomous activities where guests are on their own. The following sections and tables describe each type.

Activities Initiated by Family Member

One of the Sims under your control must prepare food or turn on the TV before visitors can join in. Turning on the TV takes a second, but you need a little prep time for a meal. It's a good idea to begin meal preparation immediately after inviting friends over.

Shared Activities

A Sim can start any of the following activities and then invite the participation of a guest.

OBJECT	VISITORS' INVOLVEMENT
Basketball Hoop	Join
Chess	Join
Dollhouse	Watch
Hot Tub	Join
Pinball Machine	Join
Play Structure	Join
Piano	Watch
Pool Table	Join
Stereo	Join, Dance
Train Set	Watch

Autonomous Activities

Visiting Sims can begin any of the following activities on their own.

Visitors' Autonomous Activities

OBJECT	AUTONOMOUS ACTION
Aquarium	Watch Fish
Baby	Play
Bar	Have a Drink
Chair	Sit
Chair (Recliner)	Sit
Coffee (Espresso Machine)	Drink Espresso
Coffeemaker	Drink Coffee
Fire	Panic
Flamingo	View
Fountain	Play
Lava Lamp	View
Painting	View
Pool	Swim
Pool Diving Board	Dive In
Pool Ladder	Get In/Out
Sculpture	View
Sink	Wash Hands
Sofa	Sit
Toilet	Use, Flush
Tombstone/Urn	Mourn
Toy Box	Play
Trash Can (Inside)	Dispose

Social Interactions

The results of various interactions are best learned by experience because of the individual personality traits that come into play. However, it helps to have an idea what each action may produce. The following table offers notes on each interaction.

INTERACTION	DESCRIPTION
Back Rub	When well-received, it is a good transition into kissing and hugging, but the Relationship score should already be over 50.
Brag	This is what mean Sims do to your Sim. Don't use it, unless you want to ruin a good friendship.
Compliment	Generally positive, but you should withhold compliments until your Relationship score is above 15.
Dance	Great activity between friends (40+), but it almost always causes a jealous reaction from a jilted lover.
Entertain	A somewhat goofy activity, but it usually works well with other Playful Sims.
Fight	Don't do it (unless you know you can take the other Sim!).
Flirt	A great way to boost a strong Relationship (70+) into the serious zone, but watch your back. Flirting usually triggers a jealous reaction from significant others.
Give Gift	A benign way to say you like the other Sim, or that you're sorry for acting like an idiot at the last party; best used with 40+ Relationship scores.
Hug	This one's always fun if the hug-ee's Relationship score is +60; a good transition to kisses, and then a marriage proposal.
Joke	Good between casual friends (+15) who are both Playful.
Kiss	The relationship is heating up, but if a jealous ex or current lover is in the vicinity, someone could get slapped.
Talk	The starting point of every friendship.
Tease	Why bother, unless you don't like the other Sim.
Tickle	Not as positive as it might seem, but Playful Sims are definitely more receptive.

CHAPTER 8:
A DAY IN THE LIFE

Introduction

Now, it's time to turn on our Sim-Cam and follow a few of our families as they handle the ups and downs of Sim life. In this chapter we switch to a scrapbook format, with screenshots of our Sims in interesting—and sometimes compromising—situations. Admittedly, we coaxed our Sims into some of these dilemmas. But it's all in fun, and we think it's the best way for you to get a feel for this amazing game.

As the Sim Turns

Our third adult roommate, Mortimer, just returned home from his night shift, so for now, his needs are secondary. We put him to work mopping the kitchen floor (the dishwasher broke last night, but everyone was falling asleep, so we figured it would keep until morning).

Five o'clock wakeup call is not pretty. Even with full Energy bars, your Sims can be a little cranky, but don't give them any slack. Get the best chef into the kitchen pronto, to serve Breakfast for everyone in the house.

Before we are accused of being sexist, we should explain that the only reason Bella is cooking for everyone is that she is the most experienced chef. If Mark turns on the stove, chances are the kitchen will burn down. We promise to boost his Cooking Skills at the first opportunity.

Switching to Zoomed Out view is a good way to manage the household early in the morning. This way you can quickly target important tasks for completion before the car pool arrives.

Mark is, well, busy at the moment. It's too bad he doesn't gain Energy points for sitting on the toilet, because he stayed up much too late last night. A good breakfast helps, but getting through the day won't be easy, and he can forget about any promotions thanks to his sub-par mood.

It's a nice family breakfast with husband Mortimer on the left, wife Bella on the right, and Bella's ex-boyfriend Mark in the middle. However, there isn't much time for chitchat, because the car pool has arrived, and it will leave at a few minutes past nine.

After canceling his thoughts about sleeping, we click on Mark's car pool. He changes clothes faster than Superman and sprints to his ride in the nick of time. Have a nice day, Mark!

Bella is on her way to the car pool and we have about a half hour to get Mark in gear, which may be a problem due to his low Energy rating. Unfortunately, Bella's Hygiene leaves much to be desired. We make a mental note to get her into the shower before bedtime tonight so she'll be fresh as a daisy in the mornin).

Poor Mortimer! We've been so focused on getting Bella and Mark to work, we didn't notice that the poor slob is asleep on his feet! We need to wake him up (he'll be so happy), and send him to bed.

Uh-oh, big time problem with Mark. He's standing in the kitchen in his pajamas, in a catatonic state. With only a half hour to get to the car pool, we need to shake him up a little and point him to the door.

We receive a reminder that Mortimer's car pool arrives at 4:00 p.m. Unfortunately we forgot to set his alarm, and his Hygiene and Bladder bars have gone south, so we need to wake him up soon. Fortunately, he ate before bedtime, so he can probably get by without a big meal.

Mortimer is up and he's not happy. With the amount of time remaining before his car pool shows up, he can empty his bladder and get in half a shower before racing out the door.

Mark is well rested, so he can fend for himself this morning. He steps into the shower as the car pool arrives, so he has almost one hour to get ready. But, while in the shower, he decides to take the day off and join Bella.

With Mortimer out of the house, we can concentrate on Bella and Mark, who have both arrived home from work. Mark socialized a little too much the night before, so he went straight to bed without any prompting.

The three housemates share a pleasant breakfast together. Perhaps they have finally buried the hatchet after the Mortimer-Bella-Mark thing. We can only hope.

Mortimer arrives home at 1:00 a.m.. After a bathroom break and quick shower, we send him straight to bed so he can party with Bella tomorrow, who has decided to take the day off.

Mark grabs the phone to invite a friend over, but before he can dial, a local radio station calls with great news. He just won §550 in a promotion!

Mark calls a friend, who says he'll be right over. While Mark changes into his Speedo, Mortimer, Jeff, and Bella enjoy a dip in the pool. That's right, Mortimer missed his car pool, too. It's a day off (without pay) for the entire house!

After dinner, Jeff heads for home. Bella and Mark retreat to the den, where Bella rubs Mark's back.

It's on to the hot tub for a long, relaxing soak. Comfort, Hygiene, Social, and Fun scores are soaring. It's too bad we have to eat and empty our Bladders or we'd never leave!

One good rub deserves a hug, as things suddenly heat up between the former lovers.

Everyone will be hungry after the swim and soak, so Bella hops out to make dinner. Soon, everyone grabs a plate and starts discussing what life will be like when they are all unemployed. Everyone, that is, except Mortimer, who prefers standing.

Mortimer takes one look at the lip-locked Sims and heads straight for the bar.

After a couple of adult beverages, Mortimer follows the lovers into the hallway where they are still groping each other like teenagers on prom night.

Bella drives off to work while our two Sim-Neanderthals take their fight to the bathroom.

Mortimer shows his frustration by slapping Mark across the cheek (he's such an animal). Bella is disgusted and goes upstairs to bed.

What will become of our star-crossed lovers?

Will Bella leave Mortimer and go back to Mark?

Will Mark feel guilty about wrecking Mortimer's marriage, and move in with the Newbies?

Will Bella reveal what she and Jeff were really doing in the hot tub?

Who will clean up the bathroom?

For the answers to these burning questions, stay tuned for the next episode of...*As the Sim Turns.*

Life with the Pleasants

One slap turns to another and seven hours later, Mortimer and Mark are still duking it out.

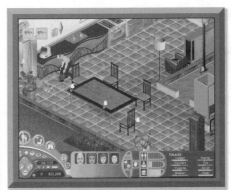

Jeff experiences the joys of working a night shift—cleaning up his family's dinner dishes...

...and taking out the trash at four in the morning.

Skeeter misses one too many days of school and gets the bad news—he's on his way to military school, never to be seen again.

Everyone is asleep, so Jeff takes an opportunity to practice his Charisma in front of the bathroom mirror. Unfortunately for Jeff, the walking dead also take this opportunity to float through the mirror and scare the •&$%$# out of him.

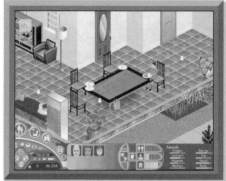

Although his icon has already disappeared from the control panel, Skeeter enjoys one last breakfast before he is exiled from the game.

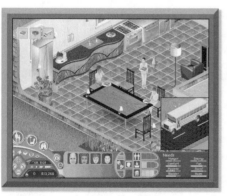

Like all kids, Daniel and Skeeter can only make snacks on their own, so someone must serve their breakfast before school.

Not wanting to follow in his brother's footsteps, Daniel hits the books and improves his grades.

Hmmm. Which pile should I pay first, the red one or the yellow one? Get a clue, Jeff—if you don't pay the red ones, they'll repossess your furniture!

Pity the Poor Bachelor

With garbage a foot thick on the floor of his house, our bachelor decides to stay outside and entertain a new lady friend with his juggling act.

The Maid should get riot pay for all the garbage this family leaves on the floor!

"Wow, she really likes me! Maybe she won't notice the garbage if I invite her inside."

Maids are limited to cleaning up Sim-messes, but that frees up the family to take care of other important needs, like advancing their skills. Diane Pleasant takes a break to bone up on her Mechanical Skills. Perhaps she can fix the dishwasher and save §50-an-hour repair bills.

"I really like you Bella, so I got you a pair of basketball shoes!"

Bachelors on a fixed budget can have a difficult time having fun. A basketball hoop in the back yard is a good investment, and if you can find a Playful friend, it's a cheap date, too.

"Excuse me, son, could you please move out of the fire so I can extinguish it?"

Kids Are People, Too

Armed with a new gas stove and absolutely no cooking ability, this bachelor decides to flame-broil the kitchen.

Toy boxes are small and relatively inexpensive. If they are placed in the bedroom, your kids can sneak in a little Fun time before school.

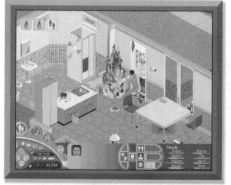

Whew, the fireman is here to put out the fire. There's only one problem: he can't get into the house because our hero is standing in front of the stove, which happens to be next to the door. We understand that the bachelor's quarters are tight, but it's probably not a good idea to put the stove next to the front door. By the time the fireman makes his way to the back door, your bachelor could be toast.

Children have fewer inhibitions, but they still don't like to use the bathroom in front of the Maid or their siblings.

Skeeter and Matthew enjoy a little Social and Fun time playing with their railroad town.

Left to their own devices, kids often stay up long past the time their parents hit the sack. In fact, even with Free Will activated, parents feel no responsibility for getting their children to bed early. So, if you forget to send the kids to bed, get ready for some serious tantrums in the morning.

Skillful Sims

Unlike the railroad, the pinball machine is a solo activity.

An exercise machine is the obvious choice for improving a Sim's Body Skill, but if you can keep your Sims in the pool, they'll increase Body scores even faster, and boost Fun at the same time.

Unlike adults, who need toys for their playtime, kids can play with each other.

Sometimes it can be hard to get your Sims to slow down long enough for serious Skill enhancement, especially if it means sitting down to read. The solution is simple: Place two comfortable chairs close to the bookcase, and give each Sim different Skill assignments. Remember that you only need one Cooking expert and one Mechanical expert in the same house. Divide reading assignments appropriately to bring their Skills quickly up to speed.

You might be concerned about an adult male who stands for hours in front of a full-length mirror in his Speedo. However, it makes sense to place a mirror in the family room for easier access. This way, your Sims won't tie up the bathroom practicing Charisma in the mirror over the sink.

Increasing the Creativity Skill through painting has an added bonus—the ability to sell your painting. But, don't get too excited; a bad painting fetches only §1 on the open market.

With minimal Mechanical Skill, repairing this shower seems to take forever, and all the while, Mark's Comfort and Energy scores are dropping. Maybe a Repairman is worth the price until Mark earns a few more Mechanical points.

As the Sim Turns: Part Two

As we return to our Sim soap, Mortimer has just returned from another night shift, and after a light snack, he decides to take an early morning swim, thinking that Mark and Bella are busy getting ready for work. After swimming a few laps, he is ready to go to bed, but wait…where is the ladder?

"I can't get out of the pool!" says Mortimer, frantically. "I'll just tread water for a while until Mark or Bella come out. If I can just…keep…going…getting tired…so tired…."

Mark and Bella finally come outside, but it's too late. Poor Mortimer, exhausted and confused, has already dropped like a stone to the bottom of the pool.

After Mortimer's body is removed from the pool, a tombstone is erected on the spot where the ladder used to be. If Mortimer were still here, he would have appreciated the humor…maybe not.

After getting over the initial shock, Mark and Bella grieve at the site where their "friend" died.

Then, they console each other further...with a dance?

"O.K., enough grieving," says Bella, as she tells Mark a real knee-slapper.

Thinking the time is right (and that they have carried on the charade long enough), Mark pulls Bella close for a kiss. But, much to Mark's surprise, Bella suddenly cools and pushes him away.

What is this strange turn of events?

Did Bella entice Mark into helping her solve the "Mortimer" problem, only to leave him in the lurch?

Find the answers on the next episode of *As the Sim Turns*, on a computer near you!

After some welcome comic relief, the two mourners console each other with a supportive hug. Right.

Sims in the Kitchen

In the Motives chapter, we provided a basic explanation of how Sims satisfy their Hunger score. As you know by now, food is readily available in the refrigerator, 24 hours a Sim-day. The supply is endless, and you never have to go to the market. However, the difference between what is in the refrigerator and what a Sim actually eats lies in the preparation. The following screens take you through the various options available to a Sim chef, and the table at the end of this chapter explains how the different appliances and countertops modify the quality of each meal.

After processing the food, Bella throws it in a pot and works her magic. Two more modifiers are at work here: Bella's Cooking Skill and the special features of the Pyrotorre Gas Range.

The snack, a §5 bag of chips, is the lowest item on the Sim food chain. It's better than nothing when your Sim is racing around getting ready for the car pool, but it barely nudges the Hunger bar.

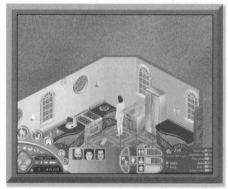

When the meal is finished, Bella places a stack of plates on the counter.

For a much more satisfying meal, direct the best chef in the house to Prepare a Meal. In this screen, Bella is getting ready to throw the raw ingredients into the food processor (a positive modifier, as noted in the table below). While one Sim prepares breakfast, you can assign the other Sims to menial labor, such as mopping or picking up garbage.

Thrilled that he doesn't have to eat his own tasteless slop, Mark grabs a plate from the counter.

Another option for preparing multiple portions is to call out for a pizza. This is a good choice for a Sim who has a low Cooking Skill. Rather than using the stove and setting the kitchen on fire, a telephone call and §40 will buy a hot pie, delivered to the door in an hour.

The Sims love their pizza, and they can't wait to set it down and grab a slice. So, don't be surprised if your Sim plops the carton down on the first available counter—even in the bathroom—and starts grazing.

How Appliances and Surfaces Affect Hunger Score

APPLIANCE/SURFACE	HUNGER POINTS ADDED TO MEAL
Dishwasher	5
Trash Compactor	5
Fridge (Llamark)	9
Toaster Oven	9 (plus Cooking Skill)
Fridge (Porcina)	12
Counter (Barcelona)	16
Counter (NuMica)	16
Counter (Tiled)	16
Fridge (Freeze Secret)	16
Microwave	16 (plus Cooking Skill)
Food Processor	32
Stove (Dialectric)	32 (plus 1.5 x Cooking Skill)
Stove (Pyrotorre)	48 (plus 1.5 x Cooking Skill)

CHAPTER 9: SURVIVAL TIPS

Introduction

The beauty of playing *The Sims* is that everyone's experience is different. When you take a serious approach to shaping your family, the game can mirror your own life. However, if you mismanage your Sims, they can sink into despair, waving their little arms in the air over failed relationships, poor career decisions, or even a bad mattress. You can always delete your family and start over. But then you would never get that warm, fuzzy feeling that comes from turning your pitiful Sims' world into Shangri La.

This chapter is devoted to the *Sims* player who wants to go the distance and fight the good fight. Because most Sim problems can be traced back to one or more deficient Motive scores, we have arranged the following tips into separate Motive sections. Although some of the information is covered in other chapters, this is meant to be a quick-reference guide for times of crisis. Simply turn to the appropriate Motive and save your Sim's life with one of our game-tested tips.

Of course, you can also take a more devious approach to satisfying or altering your Sim's needs. Our Cheats section gives you a bundle of unofficial commands to rock your Sim's world. We take no responsibility for the results. (In other words, don't come crying to us if you stick your Sim in a room with no doors and he or she drops dead!).

Hunger

Maximize Food Quality and Preparation Time

For the best food quality, upgrade *all* appliances and countertops. Anything short of the most expensive refrigerator, countertop, stove, etc., reduces the potential Hunger value of your meals. Preparing a meal quickly is all about kitchen design. Align your objects in the order of preparation, beginning with the refrigerator, followed by the food processor (figure 9-1), and then ending with the stove (figure 9-2).

Fig. 9-1. The food goes from the refrigerator directly to the food processor.

Fig. 9-2. Next stop is the stove, right next door.

Have an open countertop next to the stove on the other side so the food preparer can set the plates down (figure 9-3). Although it has nothing to do with preparation, position the kitchen table and chairs close to the stove so that your Sims can grab their food, sit down together, and boost their Social scores (figure 9-4).

Fig. 9-3. From the stove, the chef moves just a couple steps to the counter and sets down the plates.

Fig. 9-4. If your Sims are prompted to eat, they'll be ready to grab a plate as soon as it hits the counter, and with the table nearby, they can eat, chat, and make it to work on time.

Designate one Sim as your chef. Make sure that Sim has easy access to a chair and bookcase, and then set aside time each day to Study Cooking. When the resident chef's Cooking Skill reaches 10, you have achieved the pinnacle of food preparation.

Make Breakfast the Night Before

Sim food lasts for at least seven hours before the flies arrive and the food is officially inedible. If you have one Sim in the house who doesn't work, have him or her prepare breakfast for everyone at around midnight, as pictured in figure 9-5.

Fig. 9-5. After making dinner, our hard-working Sim can go to bed and sleep late in the morning.

After the food is on the counter, immediately send the Sim to bed. Most Sims should get up by 5, or the very latest, 6 a.m. to be on time for their morning jobs (the chef can sleep in). When everyone comes downstairs, breakfast (it's really dinner, but Sims don't care what you call it, as long as it doesn't have flies) will be on the counter (figure 9-6), fresh and ready to go. You'll save at least 20 Sim-minutes of morning prep time.

Fig. 9-6. It's only 5:30 a.m., but our Sim kid is already eating breakfast. After taking care of his Hygiene, he'll still have time for studying or boosting his Fun score before the school bus arrives.

Comfort

When You Gotta Go, Go in Style

A toilet is often overlooked as a source of Comfort. The basic Hygeia-O-Matic Toilet costs only §300, but it provides zero Comfort. Spend the extra §900 and buy the Flush Force 5 XLT (figure 9-7). Your Sims have to use the bathroom anyway, so they might as well enjoy the +4 Comfort rating every time they take a seat.

Fig. 9-8. Our Sim is hungry, but he always has time to receive a nice Back Rub.

Fig. 9-7. You can live with a black-and-white TV for a while, but it doesn't make sense to do without the added comfort of the Flush Force.

Rub Your Sim the Right Way

Giving another Sim a Back Rub is a great way to increase your chances of seeing Hug, and eventually Kiss on the social interaction menu. However, don't forget that it also raises the recipient's Comfort level. If your Sim's Comfort level is down, even after a long night's sleep, try a few Back Rubs. It will send your Sim to work in a better mood, which might be just enough to earn the next promotion.

Hygiene

Your Mother Was Right

One of the biggest contributors to declining Hygiene is the lack of hand washing after using the bathroom (in the Sims and in real life). If your Sim does not have a Neat personality, you may need to initiate this action. If you keep it up throughout the day, your Sim will be in better shape in the morning, when a shorter shower can be the difference between making the car pool or missing a day of work.

Fig. 9-9. This Sim has an average Neat rating, which means she won't always wash her hands after using the bathroom. A few gentle reminders are in order.

Flush Your Troubles Away

Sad but true, sloppy Sims don't flush (figure 9-10). It's easy to overlook this nasty habit during a busy day, but it could lead to trouble. A clogged toilet may not affect Hygiene directly, but if your Sim is forced to pee on the floor because the toilet is not working, the Hygiene score drops dramatically.

Fig. 9-10. Second time tonight for this soldier, and we're still waiting for the first flush.

Bladder

Sorry, there's no magic formula for relieving a full Bladder. However, to guard against emergencies and the resulting puddles on the floor, try building two semi-private stalls in your bathroom. This allows two Sims to use the facilities without infringing on each other's privacy, as pictured in figure 9-11.

Fig. 9-11. Dual stalls improve the traffic flow (and other flows) in the bathroom.

Energy

Getting Enough Sleep with Baby

Nothing drains a Sim's Energy bar faster than having a baby in the house (figure 9-12). If you want to survive the three-day baby period without everyone losing their jobs, you must sleep when the baby sleeps. Most likely, this will be in the middle of the day, because Sim babies, like their real counterparts, couldn't care less about their parents' sleep schedules. The baby will not sleep for a full eight hours; however, if you get five or six hours of sleep with the baby, you'll have enough Energy to carry out other important household tasks.

Fig. 9-12. This Sim mom is at the end of her rope, and the baby is just getting warmed up.

Kids Make Great Babysitters

It does nothing for their Fun or Social levels, but Sim kids will dutifully care for their baby siblings. When they come home from school, feed them, allow a short play period, and then lock them in the room with the baby (if you're feeling particularly sadistic, you can go into Build mode and wall them in). They usually respond on their own, but you can always direct them to the crib, as pictured in figure 9-13, (unless they are too exhausted and need sleep). Take advantage of this time by sending the regular caregiver to bed for some much-needed sleep.

Fig. 9-13. Big brother makes a great nanny.

Favorite Fun Activities

TRAIT	BEST ACTIVITIES
Neat	N/A
Outgoing	TV (Romance), Hot Tub, Pool (if Playful is also high)
Active	Basketball, Stereo (dance), Pool, TV (Action)
Lazy	TV (as long as it's on, they're happy!), Computer, Book
Playful	Any fun object, including Computer, Dollhouse, Train Set, VR Glasses, Pinball, etc. If also Active, shift to Basketball, Dance, and Pool.
Serious	Chess, Newspaper, Book, Paintings (just let them stare)
Nice	Usually up for anything
Mean	TV (Horror)

Fun

Finding the Right Activity for Your Sim

Unless your Sims live in a monastery, you should have plenty of Fun objects in your house. The trick is matching the right kind of activity with a Sim's personality. In the frenzy of daily schedules and maintaining Relationships, it's easy to lose touch with your Sim's personality traits. Visit the Personality menu often (click on the "head" icon) to review the five traits. Make sure you have at least one of the following objects readily available to your Sim (the bedroom is a good spot).

When in Doubt, Entertain Someone

If your Sim does not have access to a Fun activity, simply Entertain someone for an instant Fun (and Social) boost, as pictured in figure 9-14. You can usually repeat this activity several times, and it doesn't take much time (great for kids on busy school mornings).

Fig. 9-14. When a good toy is not around, Sim kids love to Entertain each other.

NOTE

A Sim should have at least six points (bars) in one of the following traits to maximize the recommended activity. Of course, an even higher number produces faster Fun rewards. To qualify for the opposite trait (e.g., Active/Lazy, Playful/Serious) a Sim should have no more than three points in the trait).

Social

Satisfying Social requirements can be very frustrating, especially when Sims are on different work or sleep schedules. Socializing is a group effort, so plan small parties on a regular basis. Keep a notepad with all of your Sims' work schedules, so you know whom to invite at any time of the day.

- **It's O.K. to ask your guests to leave. After you shmooze a little and boost your Relationship score, send the Sim packing, and call up a different one. Use this round-robin approach to maintain all of your friendships.**

- **Don't let Mean Sims abuse you. This can be tough to control if you're not paying attention. When you're socializing with a Mean Sim, keep an eye on the activity queue in the screen's upper-left corner. If that Sim's head pops up (without you initiating it), it probably says "Be Teased by...," or "Be Insulted by...." Simply click on the icon to cancel the negative event and maintain your Relationship score. Once you diffuse the threat, engage the Sim in simple talking, or move your Sim into a group activity (pool table, hot tub, pool, etc.)**

- **Unless you like being the bad guy, don't advertise your advances toward one Sim if you already have a Relationship with another. Sims are extremely jealous, but you can still maintain multiple love relationships as long as you don't flaunt them in public.**

Room

A Room score crisis is easy to remedy. If you have the money, simply add more lights and paintings. Also check the quality of objects in the room, and upgrade whenever possible. If your room is jammed with expensive objects, lights, and paintings and your Room score is still low, there must be a mess somewhere. A normally maxed out Room score can slip with so much as a puddle on the floor (as pictured in figure 9-15). Clean up the mess to restore the Room score to its normal level.

Fig. 9-15. It looks like someone fell short of the toilet. A mop will take care of the mess and raise the Room score.

Scan your house on a regular basis for the following negative Room factors:

- **Dead plants**
- **Cheap objects (especially furniture)**
- **Puddles (they can also indicate a bad appliance; when in doubt, click on the item to see if Repair comes up as an option)**
- **Dark areas**
- **If you have the money, replace items taken by the Repo guy.**

Cheats

Activate the cheat command line at any time during a game by pressing [Ctrl] + [Shift] + [C]. An input box appears in the screen's upper left corner. Type in one of the codes listed below. You must re-activate the command line after each cheat is entered. The following cheats work only with Version 1.1 or later of *The Sims*.

Cheats

DESCRIPTION	CODE INPUT
1,000 Simoleans	rosebud
Import and load specific FAM file	import <FAM file>
Create moat or streams	water_tool
Create-a-character mode	edit_char
Display personality and interests	interests
Draw all animation disabled	draw_all_frames off
Draw all animation enabled	draw_all_frames on
Execute "file.cht" file as a list of cheats	cht <filename>
Floorable grid disabled	draw_floorable off
Floorable grid enabled	draw_floorable on
Map editor disabled	map_edit off
Map editor enabled	map_edit on
Move any object (on)	move_objects on
Move any object (off)	move_objects off
Preview animations disabled	preview_anims off
Preview animations enabled	preview_anims on
Quit game	quit
Rotate camera	rotation <0-3>
Save currently loaded house	save
Save family history file	history
Selected person's path displayed	draw_routes on

DESCRIPTION	CODE INPUT
Selected person's path hidden	draw_routes off
Set event logging mask	log_mask
Set free thinking level	autonomy <1-100>
Set game speed	sim_speed <-1000-1000>
Set grass change value	edit_grass <number>:
Set grass growth	grow_grass <0-150>
Set maximum milliseconds to allow simulator	sim_limit <milliseconds>
Set sim speed	sim_speed <-1000-1000>
Sets the neighborhood directory to the path	<directory path>
Start sim logging	sim_log begin
End sim logging	sim_log end
Swap the two house files and updates families	swap_houses <house number> <house number>
Ticks disabled	sweep off
Ticks enabled	sweep on
Tile information displayed	tile_info on
Tile information hidden	tile_info off
Toggle camera mode	cam_mode
Toggle music	music
Toggle sound log window	sound_log
Toggle sounds	sound
Toggle web page creation	html
Total reload of people skeletons, animations, suits, and skins	reload_people
Trigger sound event	soundevent

PART II:

The SiMs™
hot date
EXPANSION PACK

CHAPTER 10:
LOVE IS IN THE AIR

Introduction

The *Hot Date* expansion pack brings *The Sims* to a whole new level of vicarious living. The depth of each Sim's personality has expanded dramatically, with the addition of interest management, daily and lifetime Relationship scores, and an incredible diversity of new interactions. This chapter will help you master all of the game's new features.

Relationships

Perhaps the most immediately noticeable change is the new method of measuring relationships. Instead of the familiar all-inclusive Relationship score, Sims now express their feelings for each other in two ways: a daily score and a lifetime score. The daily score is a measure of how a Sim feels about another Sim at the moment, and all interactions modify the daily score. The lifetime score, on the other hand, is the overall, lasting impression one Sim has toward another.

NOTE

Your existing Sims have their relationships translated into the new Hot Date Relationship scores when you install the expansion pack. Their new lifetime and daily scores are both equal to their old score, making the transition seamless.

Daily and Lifetime Relationships

In *The Sims 1.0*, Sims had only one Relationship score. They liked each other all the time, were indifferent all the time, or hated each other all the time. While this was easy to manage, it meant that you could never have arguments with your friends, because they would cease to be your friends! In contrast, now you can have a spat with your spouse, a quarrel with your best friend, or even a good day with a Sim you can't stand.

Fig. 10-1. Sims veterans will immediately notice the twin relationship bars. The top bar is the steady lifetime score, while the bottom is the more volatile daily score.

Fig. 10-2. Ahh, a lover's quarrel! In HOT DATE, your married Sims can have a spat without ending the relationship.

All interactions now have two facets, with an effect on the daily Relationship score, as well as a possible immediate effect on the lifetime score. The daily score is the rough equivalent to the old Relationship score, so look for the familiar interaction results in Sims' daily Relationship scores. Very important or meaningful interactions also have an immediate effect on the lifetime score, though this is usually only one or two points, at most.

Fig. 10-4. Because the lifetime Relationship score isn't immediately changed by most daily interactions, you can see a significant difference between the two Relationship scores in some cases.

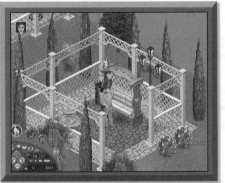

Fig. 10-3. Monumental interactions such as passionate kisses or knock-down, drag-out fights have an immediate effect on the lifetime Relationship scores between two Sims.

What Have You Done for Me Lately?

Because only a few interactions directly affect the lifetime relationship, it's more sturdy than the daily relationship, which changes with every interaction two Sims exchange. Daily relationships also decay with neglect, just as they did in *The Sims 1.0*. A lifetime relationship, on the other hand, has no arbitrary decay. Instead, it slowly migrates toward the daily score through a fairly straightforward process.

Every 90 minutes of Sim time, the lifetime Relationship score moves toward the daily score by three points. If the daily score is higher than the lifetime score at the time, the lifetime score goes up. If the daily score is lower, likewise the lifetime score drops. The lifetime score continues to migrate toward the daily score until the two are equal. If you've had a spat with a friend, make amends quickly, or your lifetime score will suffer while you are apart. Conversely, it's harder to get really high lifetime scores, as it requires constant, intensive, positive interaction.

Most interaction success is based upon the daily Relationship score of the Sims, not the lifetime score. While you have probably experienced an occasional failed interaction between your married Sims or good friends due to mood, now you must be even more conscious of your Sims' current feelings. The daily Relationship score overrides the lifetime Relationship score, so you can't always count on successful interactions between close friends.

Puppy Love

With the new daily and lifetime Relationship scores, there are now two kinds of love. A romantic interaction that happens as a result of a daily Relationship score that is over 70 inspires a crush. If the two Sims concerned also have a lifetime relationship above 70, a romantic interaction inspires love, instead. A crush is signified by a pink heart, while the red heart is saved for true love.

Fig. 10-6. Existing interactions have been expanded, with new submenus for a wide range of specific interactions.

Fig. 10-5. How sweet: Joan's first crush since high school!

New Interactions

Hot Date includes entirely new categories of interactions, which not only increase the number of ways your Sims interact, but dynamically expand *how* they interact. You now have much greater control over how the Sims behave, and more importantly, you can gain a great deal of information about the Sims you are interacting with. If you use this information carefully, you can have much more successful interactions by tailoring your actions to the other Sim's personality and mood.

In addition to the new interactions, almost all existing interactions have been expanded, so now you have a choice of exactly how to engage in a general interaction. Gone are the days when a kiss was just a kiss! Now, you can kiss on the hand, smack on the cheek, peck at the lips, or plunge into a steamy embrace that would make a sailor blush! Each specific interaction has its own criteria for acceptance or rejection, so tailor your actions for maximum success.

Been There, Done That

In *The Sims 1.0*, you could build friendships with a simple formula of repetitive interactions. Now, Sims pay attention to what you've been doing and no longer accept repetitive cycles. In every 80-minute time period, a Sim responds fully to a given interaction only once. The second time it is initiated, the Sim is indifferent, and the changes to the Relationship score are halved. If you attempt to use the same interaction a third time in any 80-minute period, the subject Sim rejects the interaction, resulting in a hit to your Relationship scores. Note that some interactions will be tolerated a total of three times instead of only twice, but it's better to avoid repetition altogether.

> **NOTE** *The only exceptions to the "three strikes" rule are talking interactions, which may be carried on indefinitely without direct penalty, and also interactions within objects.*

A new thought bubble icon represents a Sim's annoyance with repetition. You see two heads facing away from each other flashing red and black pop up over a Sim that is getting bored with a one-trick pony show. If your interactions lead to the display of the three strikes icon, change tactics and go for another form of interaction. It's more important to avoid this situation, however, because the icon means damage to the relationship has already been done.

Choosing Interactions

The new interactions can seem daunting, with dozens of choices for socialization at every meeting. The following descriptions and strategies will help you choose the right interaction with each Sim in your life. Following the interaction strategies is a pair of tables listing all of the new interactions, their criteria for success or failure, and their possible outcomes.

Available Interactions

Your Sims will have a limited number of interaction choices at any given time. This is because the available interactions are determined by your Sims' personalities, moods, and their relationships with each other. In general, Sims in good moods will have more interactions available overall. Sims with good relationships will have bolder, more romantic interactions available. Sims in bad moods and/or with bad relationships will have more negative interactions available. Personality comes into play with the *type* of interactions available. For example, playful Sims will have more entertaining and teasing options, and mean Sims will have a colorful variety of insults and attack options. For a detailed look at conditions that make each interaction available, refer to the appendix on page 218.

Ask Away

The new Ask menu is one of your most powerful tools in relationship building. Its submenu gives you all of the questions you need to find out exactly what a fellow Sim needs, wants, and likes. Use that knowledge to cater your Sim's actions to the other's liking, saving you from the embarrassment of tickling a serious Sim or talking politics to a party animal.

Fig. 10-7. Asking questions gives you valuable insight into another Sim's disposition.

The finer points of asking questions on a date are thoroughly covered in Chapter 14: A Night on the Town. However, these interactions are universally useful, and you should use them in your Sim's homes, as well. Being questioned is accepted by all but the most upset Sim. When the other Sim responds, pay attention to his or her thought bubble. It reveals the answer to the question you asked, which you can use to improve your relationship.

Fig. 10-8. Fran says she needs some food, which helps us improve her mood.

All You Need Is Love

Asking about another Sim's needs is a good way to go about improving their mood. A good mood is essential for successful interactions, so take care of a date's needs. The response indicates the Sim's lowest motive score at the time. This is completely relative, so you won't know if the Sim is at -50 across the board and happens to be -51 in hunger, or is at 95 in all scores save a 90 in bladder.

> **TIP** Use a Sim's overall behavior as a general mood indicator. If he or she isn't complaining, you probably have a basically happy Sim, and taking care of his or her most urgent need gives a good mood boost.

Whatever Spins Your CD, Baby

You can ask another Sim about their interests by selecting "Ask—What are you in to?". The response is displayed in the other Sim's thought bubble. Match the interest icons with those shown in the interest section later in this chapter, then talk to the other Sim. After you are engaged in group talk, select "Talk—Change subject." Select one of your own interests that matches the interest the Sim described, and he or she enjoys talking to your Sim more, which is reflected in increased relationship improvements. If you have no interests in common, you cannot have a good conversation.

Assault and Battery

Shoving, slapping, and fighting are going to hurt a relationship any way you look at it, but very Playful Sims who are in a good mood may actually get a giggle out of a "Sissyfight." This playful interaction is risky, as a rejected attempt has the same result as an intentional slapping. If accepted, however, it results in a boost to the Fun and Social motives, plus a relationship boost. Because of the consequences of failure, be sure you know that your subject is Playful and in a good mood before trying this!

Fig. 10-9. A Sissyfight can be a fun diversion for a couple of Playful Sims.

Teasing and Tickling

These two interaction categories are related, as they rely on the same kinds of factors for success or failure. Playful Sims who are in a good mood enjoy these interactions, while those who are not have varying negative reactions. If a Sim is both unhappy and Serious, sparks definitely fly if someone tries these interactions. Therefore, save these interactions for Sims who are Playful, and make sure they are in a good mood.

Fig. 10-10. Getting slapped is a sure sign that your joke failed.

Flirtations

Flirtation has the potential for some immediate improvement to both Sims' Social motives, as well as a bump to both the daily and lifetime relationships. Flirtation is almost a sure-fire bet when a Sim has an established crush or love relationship with your Sim, but can be risky between friends.

Greetings and Goodbyes

You can now select the method your Sims use to mark the occasions of coming together and parting company. It's important to match your choices very carefully with your Sim's relationships. If your Sims are friends, choose a friendly parting. Sims who are in love should take maximum advantage of the potential relationship bonuses by choosing a romantic parting. However, don't select a goodbye that overreaches your Sims' relationship, or it will be rejected, ending the entire engagement on an embarassing encounter.

Fig. 10-11. Even saying goodbye demands a little consideration in HOT DATE!

Hugs and Kisses

Naturally, the mushy stuff is the special playground of *Hot Date*. With no fewer than 10 kinds of hugs and kisses (and that's just standing up!), you have a multitude of ways to show that special Sim that you care. Kisses do not have to be romantic anymore: pecks on the cheek, polite kisses, and kisses on the hand all can be shared between relatively benign friends. On the other hand, a dip kiss will be accepted only by an established love interest, making it impossible to use as a love-inspiring romantic encounter.

> **TIP** *The tame kisses have relatively low requirements for acceptance, so by all means let the love flow!*

Interaction Tables

The following tables contain all relevant data for every interaction in *Hot Date.* The first table describes the general requirements (some of which are lengthy) for a successful interaction, and the second lists the effects of all possible results of each interaction. Use these tables to gauge your chance of success with each interaction. Combined with the new Ask interactions, you can potentially reduce your failed interactions to near zero.

Key

>	Greater than
>=	Greater than or equal to
<	Less than
<=	Less than or equal to

Interaction Success Requirements

CATEGORY	INTERACTION	INITIATOR REQUIREMENTS	RECIPIENT REQUIREMENTS
Ask	How Are You?	None	Mood >= -80
Ask	How's Work?	None	Mood >= -30
Ask	Invite Downtown	None	Energy >= 0, Daily >= -20
Ask	Invite Home	None	Mood >= 40, Outgoing > 9
	or	None	Mood >= 40, Lifetime > 50
	or	None	Mood >= 40, Daily >= 55, Outgoing > 5
	or	None	Mood >= 40, Daily >= 70
Ask	Let's Hang Out/Date	Hygiene > -10	Daily > 10
Ask	What Are You Into?	None	Mood >= -30
Attack	Fight	Body >= Recipient's Body	—
Attack	Shove	Body >= Recipient's Body +2	—
Attack	Slap	Body > Recipient's Body	—
Attack	Slapfight	None	Daily >= 20, Mood >= 10, Playful >= 6
Brag	Boast	None	Daily Between 0–25, Mood > 10
Brag	Flex	None	Nice >= 9
	or	Body > Recipient's Body +5	None
	or	None	Daily >= 30
	or	None	Mood >= 25
Brag	Primp	None	Daily >= 50
	or	None	Daily > 0, Outgoing > 6
	or	None	Daily > 0, Mood >= 35
Cheer Up	Comfort	None	Daily >= 65
	or	None	Daily > 55, Outgoing <= 3
Cheer Up	Encourage	None	Outgoing > 7
	or	None	Mood >= -25
Cheer Up	With Puppet	None	Playful > 7
	or	None	Nice >= 4, Mood >= -30
	or	None	Nice < 4, Mood >= -40
Compliment	Admire	None	Nice <= 3, Mood > 60
	or	None	Nice > 3, Daily > -25
	or	None	Nice > 3, Mood > 10

Interaction Success Requirements, continued

CATEGORY	INTERACTION	INITIATOR REQUIREMENTS	RECIPIENT REQUIREMENTS
Compliment	Worship	None	Daily >= 20, Charisma >= 7
	or	None	Daily >= 20, Outgoing <= 3, Mood > 60
	or	None	Daily >= 20, Outgoing > 3, Nice > 4
	or	None	Daily >= 20, Outgoing > 3, Nice <= 3, Mood > 60
Dance	Lively	None	Daily > -10, Energy >= 10, Mood >=0, Outgoing > 3
	or	None	Daily > -10, Energy >= 10, Mood >=0, Outgoing <= 3, Mood > 40
	or	None	Daily > -10, Energy >= 10, Mood >=0, Outgoing <= 3, Daily > 30
Dance	Slow	Hygiene > 20	Energy > 10, Mood > 20, Daily > -10, Outgoing > 3
	or	Hygiene > 20	Energy > 10, Mood > 20, Daily <= -10, Lifetime >= 35
	or	Hygiene > 20	Energy > 10, Mood > 40, Outgoing <= 3
	or	Hygiene > 20	Energy > 10, Mood > 20, Daily > 30
Entertain	Joke	None	Playful > 7
	or	None	Playful < 3, Daily > 30, Mood > 50
	or	None	Playful >= 3, Daily > 30
	(Mild Accept)	None	Playful >= 3, Daily >= -10
	(Mild Accept)	None	Playful < 3, Mood > 50, Daily >= -10
Entertain	Juggle	None	Playful > 7
	or	None	Playful >= 3, Daily > 20
	or	None	Playful < 3, Mood > 50, Daily > 20
Entertain	With Puppet	None	Nice < 4, Mood > 50
	or	None	Nice >= 3, Playful >= 7
	or	None	Nice >= 3, Playful < 3, Mood > 50
Flirt	Check out	None	Mood >= -10, Outgoing >=7
	or	None	Mood >= -10, Outgoing > 2, Mood > 40
	or	None	Mood >= -10, Outgoing > 2, Daily > 20
	or	None	Mood >= -10, Outgoing <= 2, Charisma >= 3
	or	None	Mood >= -10, Outgoing <= 2, Body >= 5
	or	None	Mood >= -10, Outgoing <= 2, Mood > 30
	or	None	Mood >= -10, Outgoing <= 2, Daily > 15

Interaction Success Requirements, continued

CATEGORY	INTERACTION	INITIATOR REQUIREMENTS	RECIPIENT REQUIREMENTS
Flirt	Growl	None	Mood >= 20, Outgoing >= 9
	or	None	Mood < 20, Lifetime >= 30
	or	None	Outgoing >= 4
	or	None	Mood > 50
	or	None	Daily > 25
Flirt	Backrub	None	Mood > 20, Daily or Lifetime > 35
	or	None	Mood > 20, Outgoing >= 6
	or	None	Mood > 20, Daily > 30
Flirt	Sweet Talk	None	Daily or Lifetime >= 40
Greet	Wave	None	Lifetime > -40
Greet	Shake Hands	None	Lifetime >= -20
Greet	Air Kiss	None	Lifetime >= 20
Greet	Kiss Cheek	None	Lifetime >= 20
Greet	Hug	None	Lifetime > -20
Greet	Romantic Kiss	None	Lifetime >= 50
	or	In Love	In love
Greet	Suave Kiss	None	Lifetime > 15
Hug	Friendly	Hygiene >= -40	Mood >50
	or	Hygiene >= -40	Daily > 30
	or	Hygiene >= -40	Nice >= 2, Mood > 10
Hug	Intimate	Hygiene >= -40	Nice >= 3, Daily > 20
	or	Hygiene >= -40	Nice < 3, Mood > 60
	or	Hygiene >= -40	Nice < 3, Daily or Lifetime > 30
Hug	Leap Into Arms	Hygiene >= -40	Nice or Playful >= 7
	or	Hygiene >= -40	Mood > 40
	or	Hygiene >= -40	Daily > 45
	or	Hygiene >= -40	Lifetime > 30
Hug	Romantic	Hygiene >= -40	Nice < 3, Mood > 60
	or	Hygiene >= -40	Nice < 3, Daily > 50
	or	Hygiene >= -40	Nice < 3, Lifetime > 40
	or	Hygiene >= -40	Nice >= 3, Daily > 30
	or	Hygiene >= -40	Nice >= 3, Lifetime > 35
Insult	Shake Fist	None	Nice >= 4, -30 < Mood < 0
	or	None	Nice >= 4, Mood > 0, Daily <= 20

Interaction Success Requirements, continued

CATEGORY	INTERACTION	INITIATOR REQUIREMENTS	RECIPIENT REQUIREMENTS
Insult	Poke	None	Nice < 4
	or	None	Nice >= 4, Mood <= 0
	or	None	Nice >= 4, Mood > 0, Daily < 20
Kiss	Peck	None	Mood > 0, Lifetime >= 10, Daily >= 20
	or	None	Mood > 0, Daily >= 20
Kiss	Polite	None	Daily >= 20, Lifetime > 10, Mood >= 25
Kiss	Suave	None	Mood >0, Lifetime >= 15, Daily >= 30
Kiss	Romantic	None	Crush
	or	None	Daily > 60, Mood > 40
	or	None	Lifetime > 60
Kiss	Passionate	None	Lifetime > 40, Daily >= 50, Mood >= 30
Kiss	Fiery Kiss	None	Love, Mood >= 40
Nag	About Friends	None	Mood > 40
	or	None	Mood >= 0, Nice >= 7
Nag	About House	None	Mood > 40
	or	None	Mood >= 0, Nice >= 7
Nag	About Money	None	Mood > 40
	or	None	Mood >= 0, Nice >= 7
Plead	Apologize	None	Mood > -5
	or	None	Lifetime >= 25
Plead	Grovel	None	Mood >= -15
	or	None	Lifetime >= 25
Proposition	Move in	None	Lifetime >= 60, Mood >= 45, Daily >= 85
Proposition	Marriage	Different Genders	Love, Lifetime > 80, Daily > 75, Mood > 60
Say Goodbye	Shoo	None	Daily <= 10
Say Goodbye	Shake Hands	None	Daily >= 20
	or	None	Lifetime >= 10
Say Goodbye	Wave	None	Daily or Lifetime <= 20
Say Goodbye	Kiss Cheek	None	Daily >= 20
	or	None	Lifetime >= 30
Say Goodbye	Hug	None	Daily or Lifetime >= 30
Say Goodbye	Kiss Hand	None	Nice <= 3, Daily >= 60
	or	None	Nice <= 3, Lifetime >= 50
	or	None	Nice > 3, Daily or Lifetime >= 40

Interaction Success Requirements, continued

CATEGORY	INTERACTION	INITIATOR REQUIREMENTS	RECIPIENT REQUIREMENTS
Say Goodbye	Polite Kiss	None	Outgoing >= 6, Daily >= 40
	or	None	Outgoing >= 6, Lifetime >= 60
	or	None	Outgoing < 6, Daily or Lifetime >= 60
Say Goodbye	Passionate Kiss	None	Outgoing >= 7, Daily >= 60
	or	None	Outgoing >= 7, Lifetime >= 65
	or	None	Outgoing < 7, Daily >= 80
	or	None	Outgoing < 7, Lifetime >= 65
Talk	About Interests	(always accepted)	—
Talk	Change Subject	(always accepted)	—
Talk	Gossip	None	Daily > 40
Tease	Imitate	None	Playful > 6, Mood > 50
	or	None	Playful > 6, Mood < 0
	or	None	Daily >= -15, Lifetime > 50, Playful <= 6
Tease	Taunt	None	Mood or Daily > -20
Tease	Raspberry	None	Mood or Daily >= -20, Lifetime <= 25
Tease	Scare	None	Playful >= 5
	or	None	Mood > 25
Tickle	Ribs	None	Playful > 5
	or	None	Mood > 50
Tickle	Extreme	None	Playful > 5
	or	None	Mood > 50

Social Interaction Results

INTERACTION	RESPONSE	DAILY RELATIONSHIP CHANGE	LIFETIME RELATIONSHIP CHANGE	SOCIAL SCORE CHANGE
ATTACKS				
Slap	Cry	0	0	3
Slap	Slap Back	-10	-3	-7
Be Slapped	Cry	-20	-10	-17
Be Slapped	Slap Back	-15	-7	3
Sissyfight	Cry	0	0	3
Sissyfight	Fight Back	-8	-2	-5
Be Sissyfought	Cry	-16	-8	-13

Social Interaction Results, continued

INTERACTION	RESPONSE	DAILY RELATIONSHIP CHANGE	LIFETIME RELATIONSHIP CHANGE	SOCIAL SCORE CHANGE
ATTACKS, continued				
Be Sissyfought	Fight Back	-13	-5	3
Shove	Cry	0	0	3
Shove	Shove Back	-8	-2	-5
Be Shoved	Cry	-16	-8	-13
Be Shoved	Shove Back	-13	-5	3
BRAGGING				
Brag	Good	5	0	10
Brag	Bad	-5	0	0
Be Bragged To	Good	3	0	5
Be Bragged To	Bad	-5	0	0
INSULTS				
Insult	Cry	-6	-3	0
Insult	Stoic	0	-1	3
Insult	Angry	-10	-1	5
Be Insulted	Cry	-12	-5	-10
Be Insulted	Stoic	-8	0	-5
Be Insulted	Angry	-14	-2	-7
TEASING				
Taunt	Giggle	4	0	7
Taunt	Cry	0	0	3
Be Taunted	Giggle	4	0	7
Be Taunted	Cry	-10	0	-7
Imitate With Puppet	Giggle	4	0	7
Imitate With Puppet	Cry	0	0	3
Be Imitated With Puppet	Giggle	4	0	7
Be Imitated With Puppet	Cry	-10	0	-7
Scare	Laugh	5	0	10
Scare	Angry	-5	0	0
Be Scared	Laugh	5	0	8
Be Scared	Angry	-10	0	0

Social Interaction Results, continued

INTERACTION	RESPONSE	DAILY RELATIONSHIP CHANGE	LIFETIME RELATIONSHIP CHANGE	SOCIAL SCORE CHANGE
TICKLING				
Tickle	Laugh	8	0	10
Tickle	Refuse	-5	-1	0
Be Tickled	Laugh	5	0	10
Be Tickled	Refuse	-8	-2	0
Extreme Tickle	Laugh	8	0	10
Extreme Tickle	Refuse	-5	-1	0
Be Extreme Tickled	Laugh	5	0	10
Be Extreme Tickled	Refuse	-5	-1	0
CHEERING				
Motivate	Good	5	0	7
Motivate	Mild	0	0	5
Motivate	Bad	-3	0	0
Be Motivated	Good	10	0	10
Be Motivated	Mild	0	0	5
Be Motivated	Bad	-10	0	0
Cheer Up With Puppet	Good	5	0	7 (Sensitive: 6)
Cheer Up With Puppet	Mild	0	0	5
Cheer Up With Puppet	Bad	-3	0	0
Be Cheered Up With Puppet	Good	6	0	10
Be Cheered Up With Puppet	Mild	0	0	5
Be Cheered Up With Puppet	Bad	-10	0	0
COMPLIMENTS				
Admire	Accept	4	1	5
Admire	Reject	-10	-1	0
Be Admired	Accept	3	2	11
Be Admired	Reject	-7	-2	0
Worship	Accept	3	1	5
Worship	Reject	-15	-5	0
Be Worshiped	Accept	4	2	15
Be Worshiped	Reject	-10	-4	0

Social Interaction Results, continued

INTERACTION	RESPONSE	DAILY RELATIONSHIP CHANGE	LIFETIME RELATIONSHIP CHANGE	SOCIAL SCORE CHANGE
DANCING				
Dance Energetic	Accept	6	0	13
Dance Energetic	Reject	-5	0	0
Be Danced Energetic With	Accept	6	0	13
Be Danced Energetic With	Reject	-5	0	0
Dance Slow	Accept	8	2	15
Dance Slow	Reject	-10	-3	-4
Be Danced Slow With	Accept	8	2	15
Be Danced Slow With	Reject	-7	-2	0
ENTERTAINING				
Joke	Laugh	3	0	9
Joke	Giggle	2	0	7
Joke	Fail	-6	0	0
Hear Joke	Laugh	4	0	10
Hear Joke	Giggle	3	0	7
Hear Joke	Fail	-7	0	0
Juggle or Puppet	Laugh	3	0	7
Juggle or Puppet	Fail	-10	0	0
Watch Juggle	Laugh	4	0	10
Watch Puppet	Laugh	4	0	13
Watch Juggle or Puppet	Fail	-7	0	0
FLIRTATION				
Give Backrub	Accept	3	2	7
Give Backrub	Reject	-7	-2	0
Receive Backrub	Accept	5	3	10
Receive Backrub	Reject	-10	-3	0
Give Suggestion	Accept	4	1	10
Give Suggestion	Ignore	-5	0	0
Give Suggestion	Reject	-5	-1	-10

Social Interaction Results, continued

INTERACTION	RESPONSE	DAILY RELATIONSHIP CHANGE	LIFETIME RELATIONSHIP CHANGE	SOCIAL SCORE CHANGE
FLIRTATION, continued				
Receive Suggestion	Accept	6	1	10
Receive Suggestion	Ignore	-3	0	0
Receive Suggestion	Reject	-7	-2	0
Check Out	Accept	5	2	10
Check Out	Ignore	-5	0	0
Check Out	Reject	-8	-1	-10
Be Checked Out	Accept	5	2	10
Be Checked Out	Ignore	-3	0	0
Be Checked Out	Reject	-10	-3	0
Growl	Accept	5	2	10
Growl	Ignore	-5	0	0
Growl	Reject	-8	-2	-10
Receive Growl	Accept	6	2	10
Receive Growl	Ignore	-3	0	0
Receive Growl	Reject	-10	-3	0
GOODBYES				
Goodbye—Shake Hand	Good	2	0	0
Goodbye—Shake Hand	Bad	-2	0	0
Goodbye—Have Hand Shook	Good	2	0	0
Goodbye—Have Hand Shook	Bad	-2	0	0
Goodbye—Hug	Good	5	0	0
Goodbye—Hug	Bad	-5	0	0
Goodbye—Be Hugged	Good	5	0	0
Goodbye—Be Hugged	Bad	-5	0	0
Goodbye—Polite Kiss	Good	7	2	0
Goodbye—Polite Kiss	Bad	-7	-3	0
Goodbye—Be Polite Kissed	Good	7	3	0
Goodbye—Be Polite Kissed	Bad	-7	-2	0
Goodbye—Kiss Cheek	Good	3	0	0

Social Interaction Results, continued

INTERACTION	RESPONSE	DAILY RELATIONSHIP CHANGE	LIFETIME RELATIONSHIP CHANGE	SOCIAL SCORE CHANGE
GOODBYES, continued				
Goodbye—Kiss Cheek	Bad	-3	0	0
Goodbye—Have Cheek Kissed	Good	3	0	0
Goodbye—Have Cheek Kissed	Bad	-3	0	0
Goodbye—Kiss Hand	Good	3	1	0
Goodbye—Kiss Hand	Bad	-3	-3	0
Goodbye—Have Hand Kissed	Good	3	2	0
Goodbye—Have Hand Kissed	Bad	-3	-2	0
Goodbye—Passionate Kiss	Good	10	5	0
Goodbye—Passionate Kiss	Bad	-10	-6	0
Goodbye—Be Passionate Kissed	Good	10	5	0
Goodbye—Be Passionate Kissed	Bad	-10	-6	0
Goodbye—Wave	Good	1	0	0
Goodbye—Wave	Bad	-1	0	0
Goodbye—Be Waved To	Good	1	0	0
Goodbye—Be Waved To	Bad	-1	0	0
Goodbye—Shoo	Good	1	0	0
Goodbye—Shoo	Neutral	0	0	0
Goodbye—Shoo	Bad	0	0	0
Goodbye—Be Shooed	Good	1	0	0
Goodbye—Be Shooed	Neutral	0	0	0
Goodbye—Be Shooed	Bad	-3	0	0
GREETINGS				
Greet—Wave	Good	1	0	2
Greet—Wave	Bad	-2	0	2
Greet—Shake Hands	Good	1	0	2
Greet—Shake Hands	Bad	-2	-2	0
Greet—Have Hands Shook	Good	2	1	0
Greet—Have Hands Shook	Bad	-2	-2	0
Greet—Air Kiss	Good	2	0	3

Social Interaction Results, continued

INTERACTION	RESPONSE	DAILY RELATIONSHIP CHANGE	LIFETIME RELATIONSHIP CHANGE	SOCIAL SCORE CHANGE
GREETINGS, continued				
Greet—Air Kiss	Bad	-4	0	-3
Greet—Be Air Kissed	Good	2	0	3
Greet—Be Air Kissed	Bad	-4	0	-3
Greet—Polite Kiss	Good	5	1	5
Greet—Polite Kiss	Bad	-8	-2	4
Greet—Be Polite Kissed	Good	5	5	1
Greet—Be Polite Kissed	Bad	-6	-1	-3
Greet—Kiss Hand	Good	5	1	5
Greet—Have Hand Kissed	Good	5	1	10
Greet—Kiss Hand	Bad	-6	-2	5
Greet—Have Hand Kissed	Bad	-6	-1	-3
Greet—Hug	Good	8	2	8
Greet—Hug	Bad	-8	-2	4
Greet—Be Hugged	Good	8	2	8
Greet—Be Hugged	Bad	-8	-1	-3
Greet—Romantic Kiss	Good	12	3	12
Greet—Romantic Kiss	Bad	-12	-2	-5
Greet—Be Romantic Kissed	Good	12	3	12
Greet—Be Romantic Kissed	Bad	-12	-2	-3
HUGS				
Friendly Hug	Accept	4	1	8
Friendly Hug	Tentative	2	0	5
Friendly Hug	Refuse	-5	-1	0
Be Friendly Hugged	Accept	5	1	8
Be Friendly Hugged	Tentative	4	0	5
Be Friendly Hugged	Refuse	-5	-1	0
Body Hug	Accept	5	2	10
Body Hug	Tentative	5	0	7
Body Hug	Refuse	-10	-3	0
Be Body Hugged	Accept	8	2	10
Be Body Hugged	Tentative	4	0	7

Social Interaction Results, continued

INTERACTION	RESPONSE	DAILY RELATIONSHIP CHANGE	LIFETIME RELATIONSHIP CHANGE	SOCIAL SCORE CHANGE
HUGS, continued				
Be Body Hugged	Refuse	-10	-2	0
Romantic Hug	Accept	5	2	10
Romantic Hug	Tentative	5	0	7
Romantic Hug	Reject	-10	-3	0
Be Romantic Hugged	Accept	8	2	10
Be Romantic Hugged	Tentative	4	0	7
Be Romantic Hugged	Reject	-10	-2	0
Flying Hug	Accept	9	2	10
Flying Hug	Refuse	-15	-4	0
Be Flying Hugged	Accept	8	2	10
Be Flying Hugged	Tentative	4	0	7
Be Flying Hugged	Refuse	-10	-2	0
KISSES				
Kiss Hand	Passionate	5	0	5
Kiss Hand	Polite	4	0	4
Kiss Hand	Deny	-5	-1	4
Have Hand Kissed	Passionate	5	0	5
Have Hand Kissed	Polite	4	0	4
Have Hand Kissed	Deny	-5	0	0
Kiss Polite	Passionate	6	1	7
Kiss Polite	Polite	5	0	5
Kiss Polite	Deny	-7	-1	4
Be Kissed Politely	Passionate	6	1	7
Be Kissed Politely	Polite	5	0	5
Be Kissed Politely	Deny	-6	-1	0
Kiss Tentative	Passionate	8	2	8
Kiss Tentative	Polite	6	1	6
Kiss Tentative	Deny	-9	-2	4
Be Kissed Tentatively	Passionate	8	2	8

Social Interaction Results, continued

INTERACTION	RESPONSE	DAILY RELATIONSHIP CHANGE	LIFETIME RELATIONSHIP CHANGE	SOCIAL SCORE CHANGE
KISSES, continued				
Be Kissed Tentatively	Polite	6	1	6
Be Kissed Tentatively	Deny	-8	-2	0
Kiss Passionately	Passionate	13	4	10
Kiss Passionately	Polite	8	2	8
Kiss Passionately	Deny	-10	-3	4
Be Kissed Passionately	Passionate	13	3	10
Be Kissed Passionately	Polite	8	2	8
Be Kissed Passionately	Deny	-10	-4	0
Dip Kiss	Passionate	15	5	15
Dip Kiss	Polite	10	2	10
Dip Kiss	Deny	-15	-5	4
Be Dip Kissed	Passionate	15	5	15
Be Dip Kissed	Polite	10	2	10
Be Dip Kissed	Deny	-15	-5	0
NAGGING				
Nag	Giggle	-1	0	3
Nag	Cry	-4	-1	3
Be Nagged	Giggle	-3	0	4
Be Nagged	Cry	-8	-2	-5
PLEADING				
Apologize	Accept	8	0	8
Apologize	Reject	-8	0	3
Be Apologized To	Accept	8	0	8
Be Apologized To	Reject	-5	0	3
Grovel	Accept	12	0	8
Grovel	Reject	-12	0	3
Be Groveled To	Accept	12	0	8
Be Groveled To	Reject	-5	0	3

Self Actualization: Interests

Interests have come of age in *Hot Date,* with viewable scores, additional topics, and even the ability to change them! The game contains 15 subjects of interest, as follows:

- 60's
- Exercise
- Food
- Hollywood
- Money
- Music
- Outdoors
- Parties
- Politics
- Romance
- Sports
- Style
- Technology
- Travel
- Weather

Each Sim has a set pool of points to divide among all interests. A score of 7 or more in any subject defines high interest, while a score of 3 or fewer means the Sim is relatively uninterested in that subject. Anything in the remaining range of 4–6 is regarded as moderate interest.

Fig. 10-12. Interests are now plentiful, and better yet, viewable and changeable!

Reading the Rags

You can modify your Sim's interests by purchasing a magazine at a newsstand and reading it after your Sim comes home. Each time your Sim reads a magazine, the interests related to the magazine's content rise. Because the total number of interest points is drawn from a fixed pool, other interests simultaneously fall, so you may have to juggle magazines to end up with the combination of scores that's right for your Sim.

Fig. 10-13. The magazine rack downtown lets you change your Sim's interest levels.

The magazines available in the game and the interests they increase are listed on the table below.

Magazine Topics

MAGAZINE TITLE	INTERESTS SERVED
MaxSimum	Exercise, Outdoors, Travel
Victor's Digest	Food, Sports, Weather
The Avarix	Money, Politics, Technology
Livin' Large	60's, Music, Parties
WhooNoo	Hollywood, Romance, Style

Talk Is Cheap

Conversations are much more complex in Hot Date. In the original version of the game, all of your Sims would enjoy talking about any topic. Now, they want to talk about the things that interest them! If two conversing Sims share one or more interests at a high level, talking results in maximum gains to their daily Relationship score. If the Sims have nothing in common, talking can be a complete waste of time.

TIP Use the "Ask—What are you in to?" interaction with new acquaintances to figure out what they want to talk about, then change the topic to an interest that your Sim shares. Remember, however, that you can't change the topic during regular talk.

Use the "Talk—Change Subject" interaction to steer the conversation toward a common interest or a topic that caters to a particular Sim's interests. This option is available only when your Sim is involved in an ongoing conversation. Just like talking, this interaction is always accepted, so it's a safe bet in any situation.

Fig. 10-14. The interest icons displayed above talking Sims represent specific topics of conversation.

CHAPTER 11:
OBJECTS D'AMOR

Introduction

Hot Date does incredible things for The Sims' object system. Newly sorted object lists help you shop with ease for specific types of items. You'll find more than 100 new objects in the expansion pack, including some incredible new types that offer all-new functionality. This chapter will introduce you to all of the features, stats, and functions of the new objects.

NOTE

All existing player-created objects will be compatible with Hot Date, *but they must be "re-transmogrified" to work. If you have downloaded objects in your game, get updated copies from* www.thesims.com.

Shop Till You Drop

Each object category now has special sorting options in Buy Mode, making it much easier to browse for a specific type of object. For example, instead of digging through all decorations, now you can shop specifically for rugs. This helps you easily compare prices, scores, and design features of similar objects when you're shopping.

Fig. 11-1. Handy new subcategories allow you to sort objects into specific types for easy comparison shopping.

You can still shop using the master lists, by selecting "All" at the end of the subcategory listings. However, you'll probably find it very easy to navigate the subcategory menu. It works just like the original menu: click on a subcategory to bring up a sorted list of objects of that specific type. Use the back arrow to return to the general object categories.

TIP *Hover the mouse over the new subcategory icons to learn what object type they represent. They're very intuitive, so you probably won't need the help after just a few shopping trips.*

New Object Types

Hot Date gives you much more than just a new set of objects: In this expansion pack, you'll also find entirely new *types* of objects! Long-awaited ceiling fixtures, plant boxes, and awnings add new dimensions to your Sim houses and buildings. This section takes a look at each new object type and helps you place them with style.

Ceilings: The Final Frontier

You can put objects on the floor. You can put lights on the walls. You can even put a pool in the ground. Now, at long last, you can also put things on the ceiling! This may sound pretty straightforward, but for veteran *Sim* players, ceiling-mounted lights are a dream come true. Space-saving, ceiling-mounted lighting adds form and function to large rooms with open central areas. You'll swoon over the new decorating options the ceiling objects give you, and your Sims will love you for the uncluttered floors and increased Room values.

Fig. 11-2. With the inclusion of three new ceiling lights, your decorating options have expanded to the last untouched surface of Sim households!

Fig. 11-3. Plant boxes look particularly fitting in elegant restaurants.

Ceiling lights are liberating and wonderfully useful, but they require the same thoughtful consideration that you use for all of your other objects. Ceiling objects, naturally, hang down from the ceiling and are always visible. As such, they obscure your view in certain situations, preventing you from seeing the action. Therefore, take likely Sim socializing spots into consideration when placing your ceiling lights, and keep them out of the way of potential faces and thought bubbles.

Planting Walls

Two new planter boxes give you fresh design options when planning traffic flow. The boxes, which come in indoor and outdoor varieties, are excellent for dividing up an area without making walls. This comes in handy when you want to provide a bit of privacy between booths in high class restaurants, or it can be just the thing for a stylish half wall in your home's entry. Exterior planter boxes add a dignified touch to your landscaping and spruce up any outdoor area.

A New Day Is Awning

Awnings are a wonderful new way to liven up your exteriors. Because they are objects rather than building elements, you can combine them with any wall you please: plain surfaces, windows, or even doors. They automatically wrap around corners, whether it's an inside corner or an outside corner. Awnings liven up any downtown business and can be a very homey touch over your windows back in the neighborhood.

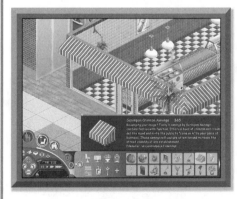

Fig. 11-4. Awnings let you bring a new level of personal touch to your home exteriors.

Getting Together

All-new levels of social object interactions are here, from a pleasant chat in the dining booths to steamy scenes in the Love Tub. Several new objects offer unique social interactions when your Sims use them together. Below, you'll find detailed explanations of all possible interactions, and tips for using them.

Following the individual explanations is a table that lists all of the possible results of these interactions, and the effects on your Sims' relationships and moods. In each table, the listed results apply to both Sims unless specifically noted in the "Response" column.

Feeding Love

In addition to several standard interactions, two special interactions are available when your Sims are together in a dining booth. Footsie is the safest play, with the lowest required scores for success. Playful Sims enjoy Footsie, while more serious Sims would prefer a more productive endeavor. You can up the ante with Cuddling, which moves your Sims closer together and brings up additional options, such as Make Out, Kiss, Embrace, and Romantic Kiss. These options are only available after Cuddle has been accepted. Cuddling increases Fun and can be a way into the heart of more serious Sims.

Fig. 11-5. Find romance aplenty in the booths of your Sim's favorite diner.

Dining Object Interaction Results

INTERACTION	RESPONSE	DAILY RELATIONSHIP CHANGE	LIFETIME RELATIONSHIP CHANGE	SOCIAL SCORE CHANGE	FUN SCORE CHANGE
Gossip	Accept	2	0	5	3
Gossip	Neutral	1	0	1	0
Gossip	Reject	-3	0	0	-1
Be Gossiped To	Accept	2	0	5	3
Be Gossiped To	Neutral	1	0	1	0
Be Gossiped To	Reject	-2	0	0	-1
Cuddle	Accept	2	0	4	3
Cuddle	Neutral	2	-1	0	0
Cuddle	Reject	-2	-1	0	-2
Be Cuddled	Accept	2	0	4	3
Be Cuddled	Neutral	0	0	0	0
Be Cuddled	Reject	-2	-1	0	-2
Hug	Accept	2	1	4	4
Hug	Reject	-4	-2	0	-2
Be Hugged	Accept	2	1	4	4
Be Hugged	Reject	-3	-2	0	-2
Make Out	Accept	3	1	7	6
Make Out	Reject	-5	-2	0	-3
Make Out With	Accept	3	1	5	6
Make Out With	Reject	-4	-3	0	-3
Kiss	Accept	2	1	4	5
Kiss	Reject	-4	-2	0	-2
Be Kissed	Accept	2	1	4	5
Be Kissed	Reject	-3	-2	0	-2
Romantic Kiss	Accept	3	1	7	6
Romantic Kiss	Reject	-5	-2	0	-3
Be Romantic Kissed	Accept	2	1	5	6
Be Romantic Kissed	Reject	-4	-3	0	-3
Play Footsie	Accept	2	0	3	4
Play Footsie	Reject	-3	-1	0	-2
Play Footsie With	Accept	2	0	3	4
Play Footsie With	Reject	-3	-1	0	-2
Admire	Accept	2	1	4	2
Admire	Reject	-3	-1	0	-2
Be Admired	Accept	4	1	7	5
Be Admired	Reject	-3	-1	0	-2

Swingers and Loungers

The English Garden Swing offers your Sims several new interactions, and these options are now available on sofas and love seats as well! In order of boldness, these interactions are Cuddle, Embrace, and Caress. Don't attempt a Caress with a Sim that you wouldn't Kiss, as the relationship score requirements are very similar. For a better chance of avoiding the shove-off, butter up your date with a few other smooth moves before you move on to petting.

Fig. 11-6. A Caress gone wrong leaves everyone feeling a little violated.

TIP *Caressing has a steeper penalty than Embracing if it fails, but they both carry the same rewards for success. Therefore, use Caress only if you've already Embraced, to avoid interaction repetition.*

Lounging Object Interaction Results

INTERACTION	RESPONSE	DAILY RELATIONSHIP CHANGE	LIFETIME RELATIONSHIP CHANGE	SOCIAL SCORE CHANGE	FUN SCORE CHANGE
Cuddle	Accept	2	0	3	3
Cuddle	Reject	-2	-1	0	-1
Be Cuddled	Accept	2	0	3	3
Be Cuddled	Reject	-2	-1	0	-1
Caress	Accept	2	1	4	5
Caress	Reject	-5	-2	0	-2
Be Caressed	Accept	2	1	4	5
Be Caressed	Reject	-4	-2	0	-2
Embrace	Accept	2	1	4	5
Embrace	Reject	-4	-2	0	-2
Be Embraced	Accept	2	1	4	5
Be Embraced	Reject	-3	-2	0	-2
Kiss	Accept	2	1	4	6
Kiss	Reject	-4	-2	0	-3
Be Kissed	Accept	2	1	4	6
Be Kissed	Reject	-4	-2	0	-3

Clean Lovin'

The Love Tub is obviously not a first date interaction—at least, not unless you're *very* successful! Perhaps surprisingly, Play has the greatest potential relationship and mood payoff, but also carries a very steep rejection penalty. Before you try this move, make sure your partner is in a very good mood, likes your Sim a lot, and is also naturally playful.

Fig. 11-7. Things can get very steamy in the Love Tub.

Wash also requires a good relationship, but caters to more serious Sims, with a payoff that is slightly lower. If your Sims are new to the bath and each other, stick to Cuddling and Kissing. Note that a Sim exits the Love Tub as soon as he or she is full of either Fun or Comfort, so don't try to take a bath with a Sim that's already enjoying high values in these motives.

Love Tub Interaction Results

INTERACTION	RESPONSE	DAILY RELATIONSHIP CHANGE	LIFETIME RELATIONSHIP CHANGE	SOCIAL SCORE CHANGE	FUN SCORE CHANGE
Wash	Accept	3	0	7	3
Wash	Reject	-7	0	0	0
Be Washed	Accept	4	1	10	3
Be Washed	Reject	-10	0	0	0
Cuddle	Accept	2	1	4	4
Cuddle	Reject	-4	-1	0	0
Be Cuddled	Accept	2	1	4	4
Be Cuddled	Reject	-4	-1	0	0
Kiss	Accept	3	1	6	6
Kiss	Reject	-4	-2	0	0
Be Kissed	Accept	3	1	6	6
Be Kissed	Reject	-5	-2	0	0
Play	Accept	4	2	8	8
Play	Reject	-6	-3	0	0
Play With	Accept	4	2	8	6
Play With	Reject	-3	-2	0	-2

Playing in the Park

The Rental Shack (downtown only) offers three unique interactions, two of which are related to the Pond (which must be purchased separately). Your Sims can rent a Picnic Basket from the shack and share a nice outdoor meal together. If you take the Picnic Basket to the beach, you have the option to Rub Oil on your date (only during the day). Your relationship should be fairly good before trying this interaction, and while it does not immediately improve your lifetime relationship, it's a good mood enhancer.

Fig. 11-8. A little tanning oil brings your Sims closer together, while blocking out the sun's harmful rays.

Your Sims can also get fish food or radio-controlled boats if the Rental Shack is near a Pond. Playful Sims prefer the boats, while more serious Sims will get more out of feeding the fish. Either way, a few interactions at the Pond increase your Sims' Fun, while adding a small amount to their daily relationship.

New Objects

Dozens of new objects have been added to the game for your decorating and designing pleasure. Chapter 6 already provides the definitive Buying Guide for all of the game's objects, and you can apply that same information to the new objects listed below. You'll find each object's picture, price, motive values, and distinguishing features in this guide to the new *Hot Date* objects.

Seating

Chairs

Touch of Teak Recliner

§179

Motives: Comfort (3), Energy (1)

Notes: Sims in the Recliner can engage in group conversations with other Sims in social seating objects

Sartori "Plasma" Stool

§251

Motives: Comfort (3)

SwivelMaster Office Chair

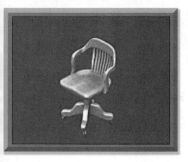

§319

Motives: Comfort (2), Room (1)

Cafeffete Iron Chair

§429

Motives: Comfort (3), Room (3)

Formi Dining Chair

§881

Motives: Comfort (5), Room (3)

Booths

Bel-Air Booth Seat

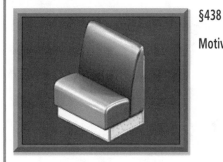

§438

Motives: Comfort (5)

Pleasario Booth Bench

§675

Motives: Comfort (6)

Notes: Downtown only

Couches

The Love Seat

§993

Motives: Comfort (8), Energy (4)

Beds

Cast Iron Bed

§399

Motives: Comfort (7), Energy (7)

Josephine Sleigh Bed

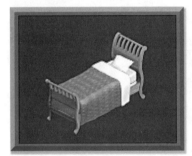

§489

Motives: Comfort (7), Energy (8)

Reproduction Antique Bed

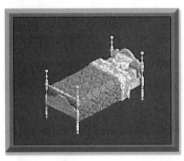

§879

Motives: Comfort (8), Energy (8)

Trendoid Bed

§1,715

Motives: Comfort (9), Energy (9)

Other

Jock Bench

§130

Motives: Comfort (2)

Ur-Bin Park Bench

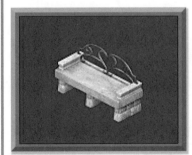

§287

Motives: Comfort (2)

English Garden Swing

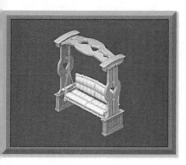

§524

Motives: Comfort (6), Energy (4), Room (1)

Hawkitol Counter

§410

Surfaces

Countertops

"UpTown" Display Counter

§191

Deluxar Counter

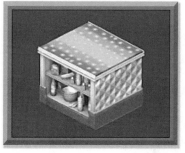

§520

"Concreta" Display Counter

§270

Notes: Downtown only

Granita Counter

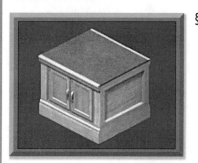

§649

Ploomies Display Counter

§710

Desks/Tables

Coffee Table 10W-40

§150

PerpetuLux-style Table

§226

Formi Table

§303

Motive: Room (1)

Modern Mission Coffee Table

§383

Cafeffete Café Table

§399

Motive: Room (1)

Survivall Picnic Table

§582

Raduchi Coffee Table

§645

Motive: Room (2)

Bel-Air Dining Booth

§699

Motive: Comfort (5)

Pleasario Dining Booth

§828

Motives: Comfort (6),
Room (1)

Power Desk

§899

Motive: Room (2)

Decorative

General Decor

Hanging Fern

§57

Motive: Room (1)

Ferby Soda Sign

§66

Motives: Room (1)

Perpetubloom Floral Spray

§180

Motive: Room (2)

Buster O'Beast

§81

Motive: Room (1)

Notes: Watch what happens when Claire the Bear sees Buster!

LunaTick Neon Clock

§239

Motive: Room (2)

Hanging Simpatiens

§87

Motive: Room (1)

Victorian Flower Urn

§250

Motive: Room (3)

Daisy Rug

§333

Motive: Room (2)

Stientjes' Windmill Whirligig

§625

Motive: Room (3)

FlatterMe Wall Mirror

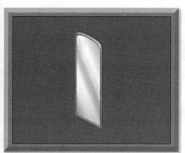

§436

Motive: Room (1),
Improves Charisma

Admiral Landgraab Portrait

§1,980

Motive: Room (8)

Antique Terrestrial Globe

§569

Motive: Room (3)

Clock Post

§2,500

"Manila 1000" Marine Aquarium

§3,999

Motive: Room (6)

Notes: Downtown only

Empire World Map

§4,112

Motive: Room (7)

Perpetual Motion Sculpture

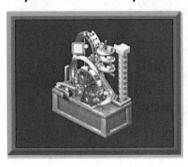

§7,647

Motives: Room (5),
Fun (4)

"IMA Irascible" Replica Model

§8,999

Motive: Room (9)

Laguna Vista Instant Pond

§9,999

Motive: Room (8), Fun (2)

Piazza Amoretto Fountain

§10,229

Motive: Room (9), Fun (2)

"Curse of Aphrodite" Statue

§14,099

Motive: Room (10)

Awnings

Scrimpon Crimson Awning

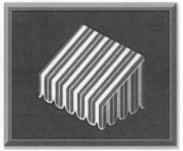

§65

Stigma Awning

§129

Planter Boxes

Faux-Boo Plant Box

§79

Concrete Planter Box

§165

Electronics

Revulcanized Eurethane Desk Phone

§89

Nonstop Noise Wall Speaker

§210

Notes: Downtown only

Audible Enlightenment Wall Speaker

§399

Notes: Downtown only

Appliances

"Light My Fire" BBQ

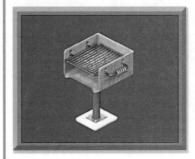

§249

Motive: Hunger (4)

Dawnette Hooded Stove

§2,488

Motive: Hunger (10)

Plumbing

Niagra Love Tub

§7,999

Motive: Comfort (5), Hygiene (2), Fun (3)

Notes: Can only be used by adults. Group activity.

Lighting

General Lighting

Street Light

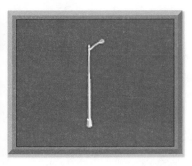

§1,100

Notes: Downtown only

Pall Mall Gas Lamp

§1,300

Ceiling Lights

Santa Baena Ceiling Lamp

§99

Radiana Ceiling Lamp

§199

"Seminary" Ceiling Fan

§240

Motive: Room (1)

Miscellaneous

MuniciSwill Trash Can

§309

Notes: Downtown only

Boggs Home Canning Center

§815

Motive: Increases Cooking Skill

Note: Can only be used by adults

"King Head" Outdoor Chess Table

§999

Motive: Fun (2), Room (1), Increases Logic

Notes: Can only be used by adults. Group activity.

Downtown Objects

The following objects are only available for purchase and placement on downtown lots. They won't show up in your neighborhood Buy screens, so go downtown to throw these new toys around.

Cash Bars

TransLight Bar Station

§4,994

Motive: Fun (2)

DTS Bar System

§5,217

Motive: Fun (2)

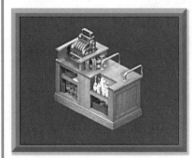

Clothing Sales

Porto-Cabana

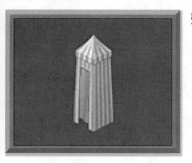

§193

Dressing Booth by VaniVille

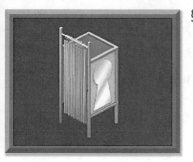

§480

Ploomies Garment Rack

§4,715

Tubula Swim Suit Display

§4,312

TresSheik FormalWear Display

§5,609

"Don't Mention It" Lingerie Rack

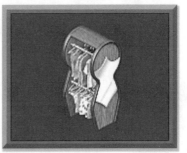

§6,800

Retail Sales

BS-PA4 Cash Register

§120

Notes: Spawns Clerks

Antique Cash Register

§310

Motive: Room (1)

Notes: Spawns Clerks

Gimble's Gamble Rental Booth

§1,787

MassPro Newsstand

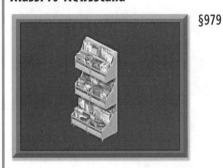

§979

Candy Caddy Candy Rack

§1,529

Confectionomicon

§2,384

"Toy With Me" Toy Display

§2,415

Floral Concepts Floor Display

§5,000

Kastle O' Toys by Magical Mystery

§3,696

Bijou Cosmorama

§5,100

Floral Concepts Flower Display

§3,699

"All That Glitters" Jewelry Display

§7,280

Food Sales

Bel-Air Series Restaurant Podium

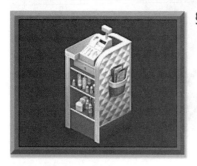

§213

Notes: Spawns a Waiter

Gastronomer Restaurant Podium

§455

Motive: Room (1)

Notes: Spawns a Maitre'd and a Waiter

Hot Dogz 2Go

§2,114

Motive: Hunger (4)

Slush Queen Ice Cream Counter

§3,444

Motives: Hunger (3)

Notes: Can only be used by adults

Cheap Eats Counter

§4,800

Motives: Hunger (4)

Notes: Can only be used by adults

Retail Signage

Florist Sign

§99

Ice Cream Sign

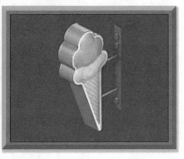

§99

Paddy Whack Dining Sign

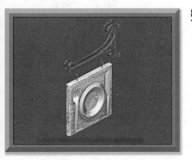

§99

Burger Clown Sign

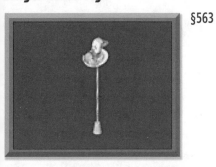

§563

Notes: Can be bought at home, as well.

Public Works

Galvanized Trash Can

§80

Stop Sign

§113

Fire Hydrant

§131

CHAPTER 12:
CITY OF LOVE

Introduction

One of *Hot Date*'s most visible new features is the addition of downtown lots. Shops, restaurants, parks, beachside resorts, and all other manner of attractions and distractions await your Sims in this exciting new area. Although it's the logical place to go with a date—or go to find one—for a little excitement, it's also a great place just to take care of a few Sim Motives, either alone or with a partner. In this chapter, you'll learn how to create a downtown area that can serve up a great time no matter what your Sims are in the mood for.

Fig. 12-1. Downtown is a new frontier for Sim architects.

Setting the Scene

When creating areas downtown, you use the same Build and Buy mode tools that you're familiar with from building your Sims' houses. However, you'll see a few differences in both form and function in the menus and objects, and downtown areas require a different planning strategy than homes. In this section, we examine the nuts and bolts of downtown building concepts.

A Downtown State of Mind

Building downtown requires you to step into a different mindset than the one you used when building homes. Your Sims behave differently while they are downtown, so use a different set of criteria for determining which items you select. Almost everything they decide to do costs money, yet they don't have to purchase the items they use. New building types and downtown-only objects further separate downtown from the neighborhoods you know and love. This section will help you make the transition from residential building to uptown entrepreneurship.

Fig. 12-2. New building concepts such as restaurants and retail stores add a whole new dimension to the game.

Feeling Groovy

While your Sims are downtown they benefit from reduced rates of decay in some Motives, allowing them to enjoy themselves for longer periods without having to attend to personal upkeep. Comfort and Energy loss are slowed, and so long as your Sims are in a good mood, they also experience a lower rate of Fun decay. Furthermore, your Sims are relieved of all concerns for maintenance, cleanup, and other household chores, allowing you to concentrate on showing them a good time!

There are some tradeoffs to downtown's Motive benefits. In particular, you don't have any way of regaining Energy downtown. No self-respecting Sim goes downtown to take a nap, so beds are out. You won't find any coffee houses, either, so Energy is probably the single most limiting factor in a downtown foray.

The downtown Motive bonuses and restrictions mean you should change the balance of your object selections slightly. Target Bladder, Hunger, Hygiene, and Room the most. Don't worry about Social too much, as you can assume that your Sims will have plenty of opportunity to max out their Social scores while rubbing elbows with all those Townies. For more information on Townies, see chapter 13 "City Slickers."

Fig. 12-3. Don't worry about finding someone to talk to in the downtown crowds!

Restaurants cater to Hunger (naturally), and dinner is a great way to add 50 or more points to a budding daily Relationship score. Comfort scores max out over dinner, as the cushy booth seats swallow your Sims in gentle vinyl softness. Provide for the meal's consequences by including plenty of bathrooms. These require very special design considerations, as they usually host several Sims at once, and traffic can become congested.

Fig. 12-4. A nice meal is one of the best ways to get to know your date.

Energy and Fun drop more slowly downtown, but they are still important. Although you can't actually increase Energy downtown, you can limit its loss. Consult the "city planning" section for tips on building areas that help your Sims move around with a minimum of wasted steps. Fun is often neglected downtown. All those dinners, bathroom breaks, and bar banter sessions don't help the ol' Fun-o-meter, so build a few Fun-enhancing objects on each lot. Make sure they are Social objects, though, so you won't have to interrupt the romance while you stock up on Fun.

Carte Blanche

Once of the most thrilling aspects of building downtown is that you have unlimited spending power! Items that are far out of your family's reach in their homes can be purchased without a second thought for use downtown. At home, you must consider the cost of each item you place, as it comes directly from your Sims' limited savings. Conversely, make style, size, and Motive value your primary considerations when buying downtown, because money is truly no object.

Fig. 12-5. Splurge on big-ticket items in your downtown lots, and allow your Sims to enjoy some of life's finer pleasures—if only for a short while.

Use the open credit account to your advantage for budding Sim households. If you can't afford that §2,500 toy, hop a cab downtown and play with it for §60. Use quick fixes like this whenever your Sims seem to be stuck in a rut with low Motive scores. Downtown, money does buy happiness!

You can spend thousands downtown on the decorative objects you've never been able to afford at home, and their strategic placement will add to your Sims' moods. Take special care to enhance the mood around areas your Sims will be taking dates. A high Room Motive contributes to an overall higher Mood rating, which makes your date more apt to respond positively to your interactions. In general, you'll find that your Sims will have a high Room score whenever they are indoors downtown.

Fig. 12-6. There's no reason to skimp on décor. Create pleasant rooms downtown to maximize your Mood scores.

New Building Elements

Hot Date includes dozens of additional building elements, including new floors, tiles, and walls just perfect for your uptown shops and eateries. In addition, you'll find a few new types of building elements, giving you additional ways to shape your Sims' world.

New Fencing

Several new dividers and fences are nestled in your building tools. Pluto's Arch is a unique column that automatically forms archways between two columns set in a straight line, two squares apart. Three- and four-way junctions can be created, allowing you to design beautiful outdoor structures, patios and breezeways, or even special indoor galleries with an elegant touch.

Fig. 12-8. Use Pluto's Arch to create beautiful indoor and outdoor areas.

The Lattice Fence and the Public Works Wall are also special linear items. When laid together, they automatically form end caps and intermediate posts, creating an attractive finished look. These walls can be used downtown to help create a sense of space and order in open areas. Plan for periodic breaks in walls, so that your Sims don't find themselves facing a long walk around a continuous wall just to get a few squares away.

Downtown-only Objects

Several of the new items included in *Hot Date* can be found only downtown, so don't despair when you don't see them on your household Build menus. All of the objects exclusive to downtown are listed in the "Downtown" section of the new object list in chapter 11, or are specifically noted in the related object category in the master list. On the other hand, several items that are primarily used downtown can also be brought home. Try the Dawnette Hooded Stove on for size in your kitchen—it may be overkill, but your Sims will definitely eat well!

Trees also sprout downtown with the addition of sidewalk planters. These special planters allow you to place trees in the middle of the sidewalks, greatly adding to the potential beauty of your streets. Place them in neat, orderly rows to achieve that special Sim City Chamber of Commerce–approved look.

City Planning

As mentioned previously, downtown construction strategy is different than building at home. This section outlines some of the specific considerations necessary for the construction of an efficient and attractive downtown.

Traffic Flow

It's no coincidence that this consideration is listed first. Even more than *House Party*, *Hot Date* features large groups of Sims competing for the same space. Huge crowds of Sims share the sidewalks with your Sims, making pathing a very important issue downtown.

Fig. 12-9. With all these Sims just finishing their meals, it can be a very long wait at the bathroom.

As you design your downtown lot, consider the sidewalks first. Your Sims enter and exit the screen at the ends of the sidewalks. If your Sims must walk all the way around your block to enter the public spaces, you'll face a great deal of congestion on the sidewalks. Bottlenecks near the entrances cause traffic jams that could leave Sims bouncing off each other as they respond to multiple impulses to move out of each other's way.

Prevent this by providing large paths (five squares wide or more) for your Sims to enter your public areas directly from the map edge. Do the same thing for your map's heavy traffic areas. Podiums, cash registers, bathroom stalls, and other important interactive objects generate traffic, causing congestion. Leave ample open space around these "hot spots," so that Sims can get around each other.

Fig. 12-10. Hot spots such as restaurant podiums can collect a crowd, so plan ahead and leave room to walk around.

A good traffic corridor is at least three squares wide—one square bigger than the proper corridor width at home. You frequently encounter more than two Sims passing through the same point in a hall or tight area, but you seldom see more than four competing for the same space at the same time. In the "hot spots" mentioned above, a four-square radius is best, even at the expense of some space efficiency.

Variety Is the Spice of Life

You'll find at least two versions of just about all downtown sales objects in *Hot Date*: inexpensive and pricey. The inexpensive models cost less for Sims to patronize but also result in a comparatively less exciting time downtown. Prepare for every contingency before your Sims hit the streets.

TIP *"Practice runs" are the only way to test your downtown lots. Take one of your Sims downtown on a date to get a sense of how well your areas work. When you are finished, leave the date through the Neighborhood screen instead of by cab. As long as you didn't spend any money, nothing will change.*

Every downtown lot (which is similar to a single house lot in the neighborhood) should serve every available Motive. Don't wait until you're on a date to figure out your new mall doesn't have a bathroom! You can customize the default lots that *Hot Date* comes with to include more sources of group activity Fun. After a few trips downtown, you might find your Sims' Fun Motives bottoming out halfway through a date.

Fig. 12-11. Sunlight on the sand, moonlight on the trees...what we need is volleyball and table tennis!

Frame Rates

Video display frame rates are a legitimate consideration when building downtown areas. Each animated object you place downtown takes a toll on your computer's video processing power. In addition to these animations, your computer also has to run the decisions and animations for every Sim downtown—a considerable task. The more animation you have on the screen at the same time, the slower the game appears to move. Unless your computer has a lot of horsepower (or if you intend to post your downtown lots on the Sims Exchange), minimize the number of animated objects.

Economics

Financial concerns are important downtown. Even though it doesn't cost you anything to build it, your Sims pay through the nose when they go downtown! Money is one of the primary factors in what a Sim can or cannot do on a date. Remember, when your Sim takes a date, everything they do together is charged to your Sim twice—once for each of them!

Fig. 12-12. Your Sims will resent you all the way to the poorhouse if you build only big-ticket attractions downtown.

Build lots that cater to more than one level of wealth. The Gastronomer Restaurant Podium is nice, but between the cost of two dinners, five tips to the musician, and a cab ride, it can break the bank for some hardworking Sims. Give them other options—hot dog stands, a Burger Clown restaurant, or some other way of satisfying their Motives besides the E-ticket ride. The same goes for retail shopping: not everyone can afford a Diamond Ring every time they hit the town.

Conversely, allow for more wealthy patrons to find something that is their speed, as well. Well-to-do Sims shouldn't have to sit through a dinner that is only moderately satisfying when they can afford the very best. Shopping should be diverse, with some low-end items for everyday dating, but also at least one high-end store for discerning tastes.

Fig. 12-13. Diamonds may be a girl's best friend, but sometimes a Lollipop just has to do.

The Big Picture

Make most of your lots present opportunities for balanced visits to downtown without having to go from lot to lot, which wastes time, money, and energy. However, your downtown should also fit together as a complementary whole. Sims have varying reactions to objects and interactions based upon their personalities. Not everyone will find public basketball court to be an attractive downtown activity, but for your Active Sims, it might be a dream come true!

> **TIP** *Many of the objects found in the previous expansion packs are incredibly useful downtown. If you're out of ideas for your downtown development, install the other expansions to send your building options sky-high!*

Tailor your lots so that your downtown can serve the varying needs of each individual Sim in your neighborhood. Take one lot and make it a paradise for Serious Sims, with outdoor chess, a library, and other thoughtful pursuits. Another lot could be the ideal place to take a Playful date, with attractions and group activity objects that will put them on cloud nine. By developing each lot with a particular set of interests or personalities in mind, you avoid creating a slew of generic, cover-all lots. More importantly, you provide real and meaningful choices for your Sims date destinations.

Fig. 12-14. Build diverse lots that cater to specific personality types for successful dates.

Building for Success

Each of the new downtown business types requires special considerations when you're building. Specific objects must be present to complete a fully operational business, plus, you must plan your rooms, spaces, and passages carefully to allow for maximum functionality.

Fig. 12-15. This cook is annoyed because he can't find a place to put down the food he's prepared.

When you're building your Sim's home, you can always sacrifice a little bit of function for form. At home, you control everyone in the house (other than the occasional guest), so you can solve traffic jams with a few simple "Go here" clicks. Downtown, however, the Sim under your control is only one of dozens of Sims going about their business. If a traffic jam develops (or someone is hogging the only space at the bar, for example), you're out of luck. Therefore, function is the most important factor when building downtown.

NOTE

All required objects for business operation must be in the same room to function. Doors and walls effectively mark the end of a room for these purposes, so leave the entry to your kitchens open for the waiters.

Restaurants

Restaurants require the most complex set of objects to operate. You need at least one of each of the following in your restaurant before the health inspector will sign off on your food permit.

- **Host podium**
- **Seats and tables for eating**
- **Stove**
- **Open countertop near stove**
- **Dishwasher**
- **Refrigerator**

Traffic flow near your podium is very important, as eating is one of the favorite activities of downtown NPCs. Leave three to five squares of open space around your restaurant podiums to allow for maximum flow to and from the podium. Your host leaves the podium to seat patrons, and crowding can get so bad that seating stops if the host cannot squeeze back to his or her post.

Fig. 12-16. Hey! That guy cut in line

Seating is the next most important concern in restaurants. This is where most of your date interactions take place, as a meal is one of the best ways to quickly boost your daily Relationship score with your date. Booth seating is desirable, because it allows your Sims to cuddle with each other during the meal.

Provide your Sims with comfortable seating, so their Comfort Motives are well served. Meals can last several hours of Sim time, so make the most of their experience. Max out your Room score around the tables with ample decorations and good lighting. With Hunger, Comfort, Room, and Social guaranteed to be at high scores during dinner, your Sims have the best chance at maintaining a good mood. As a result, they have more successful mood-dependant interactions.

Fig. 12-17. Don't try this at home: a little ambiance goes a long way. A lot of ambiance must go even further, right?

When adding décor, remember the seating arrangements during meals. Avoid placing objects where they obstruct your Sim's faces or thought bubbles. Such obstructions lead to frustration when you cannot see the important cues your Sim's date is giving you. Also, you cannot enter Build mode while on a date, so you're stuck with the offending objects until after the date. Hanging plants and ceiling lights are the most common obstructions, but you can also get into trouble with wall objects such as paintings, sconces, and of course the infamous Mood Moose.

Shops

Downtown retail shops sell a great number of specific gifts for the delight of some lucky Sim. Now you've got to go out and buy those trinkets and treasures! Shops require only two elements to work properly, as follows:

- **Cash register**
- **Sales rack or display**

Of course, it's nice to have more than one sales rack. Several varieties of each kind of retail display are available, although some sell the same type of items. Mix and match your retail displays for the best visual appearance, but as with restaurants, keep your shop's hot spots in mind. The cash register is a focal point, as are the entrances and exits to your shop. Standing displays can also be roadblocks, so either place them against walls or provide ample aisle space.

Fig. 12-18. Leave plenty of space for shoppers to browse between your retail displays.

TIP *One register can cover several "stores" if they are in the same continuous room. However, don't skimp on registers; don't make your Sims walk far to complete their purchases.*

Bars

Bars are one of the easiest businesses to create downtown, as they require only a single specialized object—one of the special downtown cash bars—plus an associated counter. However, they are quite possibly the hardest to build *right* as their special traffic demands and popularity with the NPCs make them very crowded hot spots.

• **Bar**

• **Counter**

The hard part comes in planning for the substantial traffic your bar will generate. You may find a dozen Sims ponied up to the bar at once, making ordering a nightmare. Build long bars—at least six countertops laid in a line. Box your bartenders in with a side counter so that patrons can't get behind the bar and block access to the cash register.

Fig. 12-19. Make sure the bartender has unfettered access to the cash register, or no drinks can be made.

You also can create tables in your bar, which spawns a barmaid for table service. Use the standard restaurant booths or any mix of dining tables and chairs you prefer. Create a completely open space between the seating area and the bar, where the barmaid can return for the drinks ordered by seated Sims. The traffic corridor should be almost as wide as the bar itself and provide direct access to all of the tables.

CAUTION

If the route from the bar seating to the service bar is too small, the barmaid will get slowed down by counter patrons, slowing her service to a crawl. Keep that path clear to keep the drinks coming!

Parks

Parks and recreational areas are a great way for your Sims to spend some quality time together. Active Sims enjoy attractions such as basketball courts, swimming pools, and other athletic activities, while Lazy Sims can spend a quiet afternoon on a picnic blanket or an English Garden Swing. There are no specific requirements for building a park, but the following items provide your Sims with something to do besides watching grass grow.

• **Rental Shack**

• **Pond**

• **Basketball hoop**

• **Swimming pool**

• **Park bench, garden swing**

• **Barbecue and picnic bench**

• **Restaurant in the park, food vendors**

• **Bathroom facilities**

Don't forget to attend to your park's Room score. Ample landscaping creates an idyllic outdoor location for your Sims. Fountains and statues add visual appeal, but use these in moderation to avoid a cluttered look. Several types of lights are appropriate for a park, and they are vital for preserving your Room score after the sun goes down.

Fig. 12-20. Several choices of municipal lights can illuminate nighttime park liaisons.

Fig. 12-21. The video game parlor is a good source of Fun.

Parks must serve all of your Sims' needs, just like any other lot. Either combine the park with traditional buildings on opposite sides of the lot, or make the entire lot a green space and include some portable vendors. A small outdoor café can be just the right thing for a bite to eat while in the park, and cooks can use any of the cooking appliances available in the downtown Buy menu to prepare meals.

Other Attractions

Some less obvious establishments make perfect sense downtown. Video game arcades, dance clubs, libraries, or even health spas can all be created to cater to your Sims' every desire. Anything you can imagine with the objects in the game can be constructed, and the incredible number of wall and floor patterns lets you create a limitless variety of environments. Just make sure your Sims have something meaningful to do. Include group activity objects that allow your Sims to improve their relationships while simultaneously catering to one or more Motives.

The Love Nest

Downtown isn't the only place that benefits from the new objects included in *Hot Date*. Your Sims can also enrich their homes with many of the new objects and building elements. The centerpiece of these, of course, is the Niagra Love Tub. Within its obfuscating waters, your Sims can have some frisky fun as they wash, whisper, and wiggle the night away!

Fig. 12-22. Up the ante with a date in the Love Tub.

More practical projects are also augmented at home, too. The new fence and column items give your wealthy Sims a whole new way to express themselves. All of your households benefit from the expanded wall and floor selections. The bay window, described earlier, can be a space-saving addition to a house, as well as a dramatic feature to help break up the flat exteriors of many Sim abodes.

The ceiling lights are a wondrous new addition to your objects arsenal, allowing object placement on the ceiling for the first time ever. These lights allow you to create larger rooms without suffering from dim lighting in the middle spaces. Avoid placing ceiling lights where they obstruct your view of seating or floor space that your Sims commonly occupy.

Fig. 12-23. Ceiling lights give you new lighting options at home.

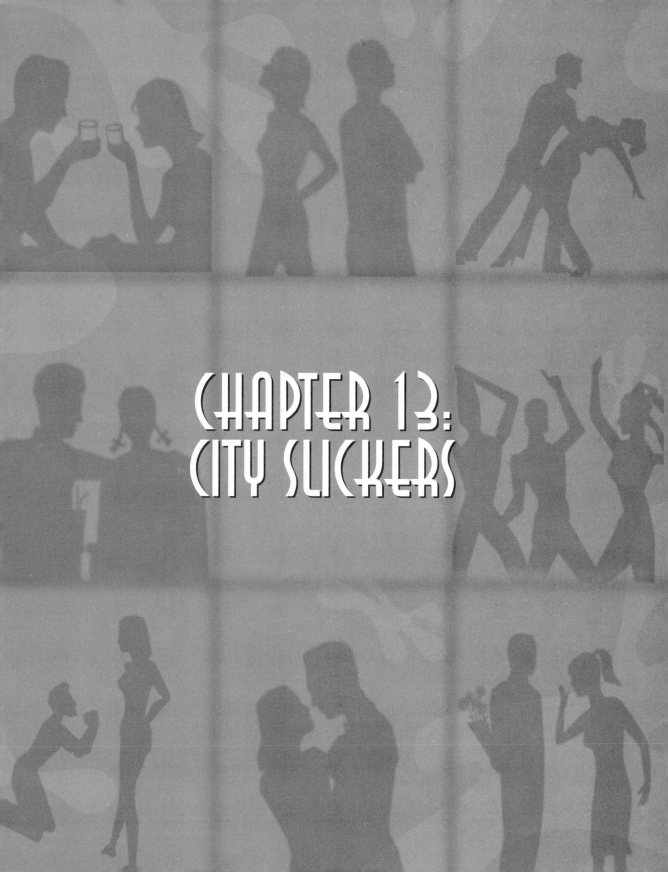

CHAPTER 13:
CITY SLICKERS

Introduction

Hot Date introduces the largest group of Non-Player Characters (NPCs) ever packed into a Sims expansion pack. You'll meet three basic types of Sims downtown: randomly generated NPCs, the infamous NPC archetypes, and service industry attendants. The downtown sidewalks sizzle with this newly expanded cast of characters! This chapter helps you figure out who's who, and just might give you a leg up in getting one of those NPCs to go home with your Sim!

Fig. 13-1. After you've established a relationship with a random NPC downtown, he or she is saved, so you can meet again.

The Bride of Frankensim

An endless cast of randomly generated characters shows up downtown. These NPCs are generated by mixing and matching the bodies and outfits from your skins folder, a bit like something out of Frankensim's workshop. Their personalities, interests, and even moods are also randomized, so you can have absolute confidence that Mr. or Ms. Right *really is* out there, or at least will be someday! So, if at first you don't succeed, try again.

Your randomly generated Sims are looking for love in the downtown restaurants, shops, and parks, just waiting for the right Sim to introduce Simself! All NPC Sims are generated when the game starts, and they are a permanent part of your game. Whenever you establish a relationship with an NPC Sim, they will show up in your relationships bar. At this point, you can call them on the telephone from home, allowing you to have an ongoing relationship.

Sim Studs and Sim Sweethearts

In addition to randomly generated Sims, you'll find six NPC "archetypes" plying the boulevards, boardwalks, and back alleys of your Sims' downtown. This motley cast of characters ranges from the suave Lover to the reclusive Wallflower. These archetypes use the same personality and interest matrix that every Sim in the game uses, but are manually set to create a very specific kind of personality that you're guaranteed to find in the game.

Fig. 13-2. It doesn't take very long to spot the Sim archetypes downtown— pay attention to their names.

Interacting with these archetypes can be especially fun, because they are all created to have interesting or even challenging personality traits. Each archetype comes in both male and female incarnations, with very slight differences between them. Below, you'll find summaries of each personality archetype.

The Hottie

This Sim is hot! Find these Sims on the arms of those who can treat them to the life they'd like to be accustomed to. The Hottie is vibrant and lively when it comes to having fun, but strangely absent when it's time to do the dishes or take out the trash. Of course, if you bring this Sim home, it's mostly for the eye candy, so contract for maid service if you plan on proposing to this siren.

Personality Traits
• **Outgoing**
• **Lazy**
• **Nice**

Preferred Interactions
• **Compliment—Admire**
• **Brag (Male only)**
• **Primp (Female only)**

Career
• **Male: Journalism—Papparazzi**
• **Female: Journalism—Papparazzi**

Names

GENDER	LIGHT SKIN	MEDIUM SKIN	DARK SKIN
Male	Woody	Fabio	Ambrose
Female	Lola	Carmen	Yvette

Interests

HIGH (7 OR GREATER)	MODERATE (4-6)	LOW (3 OR LESS)
Travel	60's	Politics
Money	Weather	Sports
Style	Music	Outdoors
Romance	Food	Exercise
Hollywood	Parties	Technology

The Lover

The Lover has the moves to make Sims swoon. This Sim's natural charm and guile are sure to win the hearts of Sims that catch his or her eye, and a promising career in medicine gives the Lover a ready supply of cash for indulging his dates. The Lover is more than friendly, but he or she likes to cut through the pleasantries and get right down to serious Footsie underneath the table—or underneath the bubbles in the Hot Tub!

Personality Traits
• **Outgoing**
• **Nice**
• **Serious**

Preferred Interactions

- **Greet—Kiss Hand**
- **Give Gift—Roses**

Career

- **Male: Medicine—Intern**
- **Female: Medicine—Intern**

Names

GENDER	LIGHT SKIN	MEDIUM SKIN	DARK SKIN
Male	Giorgio	Juan	Hector
Female	Camelia	Juanita	Lucille

Interests

HIGH (7 OR GREATER)	MODERATE (4-6)	LOW (3 OR LESS)
Travel	Money	Politics
Music	60's	Sports
Style	Weather	Outdoors
Romance	Food	Exercise
Hollywood	Parties	Technology

The Romantic

Despite the feminine connotations of the archetype name, this dating disaster comes in male and female varieties. The Romantic is romantically minded, but runs hot and cold. With a withdrawn, mysterious personality, he or she easily fosters a crush. However, this Sim's selfish side soon shows through in an extended interaction. The challenge of dating this show pony can be absolutely exhilarating, but steer clear if you don't want your Sim's heart to get broken.

Personality Traits

- **Shy**
- **Lazy**
- **Mean**

Preferred Interactions

- **Flirt—Backrub**
- **Dance—Slow**

Career

- **Male: Hacker—Hacker**
- **Female: Paranormal—Hypnotist**

Names

GENDER	LIGHT SKIN	MEDIUM SKIN	DARK SKIN
Male	Max	Jacques	Zeus
Female	Violet	Celeste	Zara

Interests

HIGH (7 OR GREATER)	MODERATE (4-6)	LOW (3 OR LESS)
Music	Travel	Politics
Outdoors	Money	Weather
Parties	60's	Sports
Style	Food	Exercise
Romance	Technology	Hollywood

The Flirt

You know the type: a little cheesy, a little forward, and maybe even a little greasy. The Flirt is all about style—yesterday's style. Just the same, this poor soul means well, and you could have quite an adventure dating this Sim. Of course, if your Sim actually responds positively to the Flirt's outrageous flirtations, the date could very well stall. After all, it's pretty likely that the Flirt has never actually been given the green light! For pity, for pleasure, or for pure fun, give the Flirt a go for a date worthy of your scrapbook.

Personality Traits

- **Outgoing**
- **Sloppy**
- **Fun**

Preferred Interactions

- **Flirt—Check Out**
- **Flirt—Suggestion**

Career

- **Male: Entertainment—Stunt Double**
- **Female: Entertainment—Stunt Double**

Names

GENDER	LIGHT SKIN	MEDIUM SKIN	DARK SKIN
Male	Randy	Humbert	Chester
Female	Betty	Emmanuel	Chantal

Interests

HIGH (7 OR GREATER)	MODERATE (4-6)	LOW (3 OR LESS)
Hollywood	Travel	Politics
Style	Money	Sports
Music	60's	Outdoors
Parties	Weather	Exercise
Romance	Food	Technology

The Partier

Ahh, the life of hedonistic pleasure! The Partier lives for the nightlife. This Sim is your match made in heaven if you are a *House Party* fanatic. Fun is the Partier's middle name, and he or she can't get enough of it. Treat Party Sims to entertaining diversions for a successful date, and stay away from discussions about anything serious. The Partier also makes an easy friend, as it is relatively easy to keep the relationship going with simple diversions that cater to fun.

Personality Traits

- **Outgoing**
- **Nice**
- **Fun**

Preferred Interactions

- **Talk—Gossip**
- **Tickle—Ribs**

Career

- **Male: Musician—Lounge Singer**
- **Female: Musician—Lounge Singer**

Names

GENDER	LIGHT SKIN	MEDIUM SKIN	DARK SKIN
Male	Trip	Rudy	Cliff
Female	Blaze	Gloria	Fanny

Interests

HIGH (7 OR GREATER)	MODERATE (4-6)	LOW (3 OR LESS)
60's	Travel	Politics
Music	Money	Weather
Parties	Sports	Outdoors
Style	Food	Exercise
Hollywood	Romance	Technology

The Wallflower

The Wallflower (or Nerd) is the shy, sensitive type. An honest career behind a law enforcement desk firmly establishes this Sim's serious side. Compassion, loyalty, and generosity are this Sim's hallmarks, which can send some into orbit, but bore others to tears. The Wallflower can be a wonderful mate, but can make a difficult date if you're not ready to spend a lot of quality time just talking and taking care of needs. Don't blow your cash on entertainment that will be lost on your date. Just make sure you do your homework with a little reading in *The Avarix* magazine before you ask the Wallflower out.

Personality Traits

- **Shy**
- **Nice**
- **Serious**

Preferred Interactions

- **Plead—Apologize**
- **Cheer Up—Sensitive**

Career

- **Male: Law Enforcement—Desk Sergeant**
- **Female: Law Enforcement—Desk Sergeant**

Names

GENDER	LIGHT SKIN	MEDIUM SKIN	DARK SKIN
Male	Ernest	Ernesto	Cecil
Female	Grace	Lily	Dawn

Interests

HIGH (7 OR GREATER)	MODERATE (4-6)	LOW (3 OR LESS)
Travel	Money	Sports
Politics	60's	Music
Weather	Food	Exercise
Outdoors	Romance	Parties
Technology	Hollywood	Style

Service with a Smile

Not all of the Sims you meet downtown are datable. All of the NPCs in the service industry (at restaurants, bars, retail stores, and other types of service-related jobs) are off limits—they're too busy working to pay attention to your Sim's advances. However, you still can have various interactions with service industry employees, many of which are completely new to *Hot Date*. In the following sections, you'll learn how and when to interact with your friendly downtown service Sims!

Food Service Sims

Hunger is one of the motives you can manage while downtown, and it's a good way to spend time with your date. All of your food is served by NPC service Sims, and additional NPCs work as support staff for the restaurant, from cooks to busboys to janitors. In this section, we take a look at what each NPC offers in the food industry.

The Waiter

The Waiter comes with both the Bel-Air Series Restaurant Podium and the Gastronomer Restaurant Podium. You can speak with him to order food, and once you've decided on a meal, he leads you to a table. To order food, select "Order Food" from the waiter's podium. There are no special interactions with the waiter other than ordering food.

The Maitre'd

The Maitre'd is spawned by the Gastronomer Restaurant Podium, and will seat you at his finest table (or so he always says) whenever you decide you'd like a bite to eat. His prices are higher than those of the Waiter, but his food also satisfies hunger better than that served up in the less expensive restaurants. After you have been seated, the Waiters in the establishment take over your service.

The Minstrel

The Minstrel also comes with the Gastronomer Restaurant Podium, and he has a few special interactions. As your dinner progresses, the Minstrel wanders around the restaurant, playing a guitar. If he plays at your table, he expects a tip. A tip costs 5 Simoleans, and must be conducted as a social interaction with the Minstrel.

NOTE

If there is a piano in the restaurant the Mistrel is replaced by an NPC pianist.

CAUTION

If you choose to go to a fancy restaurant, factor in §25 in tips for the Minstrel. At some point he's guaranteed to stop by your table, and the cost of having him repeatedly mock you is far worse than spending §25 in tips.

Each time you tip him after he plays and bows, you gain five points in your relationship with the Minstrel. If you don't, your relationship goes down by five points. If your net relationship with him is greater than 20, he lays down his guitar in favor of a violin that's sure to impress your date. However, if your cumulative relationship with him is at -15 or lower, things turn ugly. He ditches the music and whips out a hand puppet instead—which he uses to mock you right in front of your date!

Fig. 13-3. If the Minstrel doesn't like you, you can't show your face in the fancy restaurants without being mocked!

All of your interactions with the Minstrel affect the flow of your date. Requesting a song results in a small boost to your Fun motive, up to a maximum score of 23. The following table lists the effect of each of the interactions on your date's mood, and your relationship with him or her.

Minstrel Interaction Results

INTERACTION	SOCIAL	DAILY RELATIONSHIP	LIFETIME RELATIONSHIP
Play Guitar	5	3	1
Play Violin	6	4	2
Mock with Puppet	-5	-5	-2

The Bartender

The Bartender is linked to any of the bar objects placed downtown and serves all drinks ordered at the bar. You may have to wait in line when the bar is crowded, but you'll be served in turn. No interactions are available with the Bartenders themselves.

The Barmaid

When a room contains both a bar and one or more tables with chairs, a Barmaid is spawned. If you are sitting at a one of these tables, you may click on the Barmaid and order a drink. Your Sim stays seated, and the Barmaid comes over, takes your drink order, retrieves it from the bar, then delivers it to your table.

Fig. 13-4. If the Barmaid is across the room when you order, she comes over to your Sims, so they can continue their date uninterrupted.

This is an excellent way to patronize a bar, as your Sims benefit from the comfort of sitting while they wait for and enjoy their drinks. If you are sitting in a booth with a date, you have opportunities to flirt at the table, taking advantage of the mood-enhancing bonuses the bar drinks convey.

The Chef

Chefs dutifully man the restaurant kitchens, being spawned by stoves, ovens, or any other permanent cooking fixture. There aren't any interactions to be had with the Chefs, although they do prepare your food. Watch the Waiter after he leaves your table with your order, then observe as the Chef prepares your food. If you see any sanitation violations, you can pass on the food. Just don't expect to be reimbursed.

The Busboy

The Busboy is spawned by a dishwasher and buses the tables. Busboys have a continuous workload, so they don't have time to stop and chat. As such, no interactions are available with the Busboys.

The Janitor

Janitors are a staple of any downtown lot, and they appear automatically. Although they do not provide you with any direct interaction, they can be anything from an amusement to a nuisance as they go from room to room cleaning, oblivious to the activities of the Sims around them. Avoid trapping a Janitor in a hallway or room you want to use, or your downtown outing could stall as you and your date try to get around the sanitation engineer.

Retail Reps

Hot Date features new retail clerks, who provide you with cashier, sales, and even rental services at various downtown locations.

Cashiers

Cashiers are fairly straightforward. Shop among their racks and displays, and after you've selected something for purchase, your Sim takes the item to the register and pays the Cashier. Other than that, Cashiers are generally uninterested in helping you shop (does art imitate reality?). Watch out for that right forearm—many Cashiers suffer from a chronic case of the sniffles!

NOTE

Smart criminals don't mix business with pleasure, so don't expect your petty thief to pull off shoplifting. Criminal masterminds have to pay for their selections in the stores just like other Sims when they are on dates, saving the larceny for when they're "on the job." So relax, have fun, and spend a few of those hard-stolen Simoleans on your date!

Rental Shack Attendant

Rental Shack Attendants intermittently man the equipment rental facilities in parks and near waterfronts. He's a voyeur, slow on the uptake, and quick to take a break. Click on the shack to rent equipment, and he'll give it to you when he gets around to it.

The Funny Farm

A few characters wander around town with nothing else to do but engage in that "Comedic Mischief" that you see referred to on the ESRB rating on your Sims box. Not all of them have interactions available, but all are worth watching (or avoiding!) when you see them.

The Tragic Clown

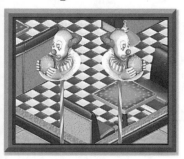

Although he was first introduced with the first Sims expansion pack, the Tragic Clown's saga continues in *Hot Date*. You may be lucky enough to see him wandering around downtown

while you are out and about. If he happens to come across a Burger Clown sign, watch his reaction! The Tragic Clown used to have an unmentionably close affiliation with Burger Clown Partnerships Incorporated, but that relationship was ended abruptly. The Tragic Clown has never fully recovered….

The Old Prude

Old Mrs. Crumplebottom is the widow of famed philanthropist and puppeteer Robert Crumplebottom. She spends her twilight years roaming the streets and shops of downtown, complaining about newfangled ways and loudly protesting the conduct of the latest generation of Sims. Nothing gets her goat faster than a public display of affection, her radar spots a kiss a mile away. If your Sims are getting fresh anywhere near the Old Prude, expect a thrashing from her purse in short order!

NOTE

While the purse-whipping your Sims receive at the hands of the Old Prude doesn't have any specific effects on mood or relationship, it does carry the indirect penalty of taking up time on your date. Because motives go down over time and you can't replenish some of them downtown, an interaction with the Old Prude detracts somewhat from the evening's potential.

Claire the Bear

Claire the Bear is the first persistent animal character in The Sims, and she was worth the wait! You can encounter her downtown and at home as well.

Fig. 13-5. An encounter with Claire while on a picnic is amusing, but nip it in the bud if you want keep your date from freaking out.

At home, things get even more amusing. Claire wanders the neighborhood in search of food in the trash. If she happens to mosey past a Buster O'Beast stuffed toy, she tries to start up a conversation with her fellow bear! Finally, if Claire sees a bearskin rug (available in the *House Party* expansion pack), she'll cry over the remains of her relative! Poor bear....

CHAPTER 14:
A NIGHT ON THE TOWN

Catching a cab downtown and mixing it up with your fellow Sims brings all the new elements of *Hot Date* together in one big package. A veritable social smorgasbord awaits your Sims in the shops, restaurants, and attractions of the city. This chapter helps you bring all of the elements of the game together and apply them toward showing your companion a world-class date.

Anatomy of a Date

First, a downtown outing together doesn't have to be about romance. You can head uptown with a buddy, a friend, or even alone. You can ask someone to hang out with you, instead of dating. All of the interactions are the same, but just like with your Sims relations at home, you can simply steer the outing toward fun and friendship instead of love and romance.

> **TIP** There is actually no functional difference between "hanging out" and "dating," although the distinction is clearly very important for role-playing. The requirements are the same for success, and once the outing has begun, the game doesn't make a distinction between the two.

Having said that, this section focuses on the romantic date (after all, the title of the game isn't *Hot Hang-Out*). There are several distinct components of a full, successful date, listed below.

- **Get ready**
- **Get a date**
- **Get downtown**
- **Share one or more activities with each other**
- **Optional: Go home together**
- **Say goodbye**

Below, we'll go over each of these components, and discuss strategies for making each step of your date as successful as possible.

The Hot Date

This section walks you through all aspects of a successful date from beginning to end. You'll learn how to prepare, when to go, who to ask and how to ask them, and of course all of the finer points of getting your way into your date's heart. Heart! Not pants; *heart!* Of course, for getting into your date's pants, see the dressing booth.

Your Sim

Getting a Sim ready to be his or her best on a date requires thoughtful planning. There's much more to a successful date than simply putting bodies in close proximity. Mood plays a heavy role in the duration of the date and the success of each interaction. Because a date's success is entirely based upon the ambiguous sum of the interactions you have with your partner over its course, a slew of bad interactions results in a bad date.

Fig. 14-1. Jim Sim gets ready for a day on the town.

If you get downtown only to find you've got no Energy, you're out of luck. Your Sim quickly tires, and without any way of recovering Energy downtown, you're forced to head home. The same goes for any other Motive score—try to leave the house with maximum values, so that you can concentrate on your date instead of satisfying low Motives.

NOTE

Because mood is an aggregate of all Motive scores, low Energy brings the date down overall in addition to limiting its length. You can get a fix for other Motives while you're downtown, but if your Sim is tired, you're truly stuck.

A healthy appetite is fine before stepping out, because a meal is one of the best ways to spend time on a date. Energy is impossible to recover downtown, and although it decays more slowly than at home, it's a nonrenewable resource. Therefore, your Sim's Energy is the ultimate limiting factor on any date, so always start your date with the highest Energy level you can muster.

The best way to go downtown is to take a day off work, and go in the morning. Have your Sim wake up, go to the bathroom, shower or bathe, then head right out. Go to bed the previous evening with a good Fun Motive by playing just before bed. After this morning routine, your Sim should be well rested, comfortable from a long night's sleep, clean, and hungry.

Fig. 14-2. Just home from work, this poor Sim is just too tired to indulge in downtown's nightlife.

Your Date

There are three basic ways to get a date:

- **Ask a housemate or visitor**
- **Call a friend or acquaintance**
- **Randomly meet someone downtown**

Each method has the same requirements for acceptance of the suggestion, but you'll have the most success with the first two choices. This is because your Sims naturally have stronger relationships with the Sims they live with, while you're likely to have a zero Relationship score with someone you meet downtown.

> **TIP**
> A Sim will accept a proposal to date or hang out if his or her daily Relationship score is greater than or equal to 10.

Remember, this is a rule of thumb, and not an actual rule. You may run into your own housemates downtown, friends from the neighborhood, or NPC Sims that you've established strong relationships with in the past. Obviously, you'd have an easier time convincing one of these Sims to go on a date with you than you'd have with a Sim you don't know.

The Proposition

You can ask anyone in your house to go downtown with you via the Ask conversation menu. If your suggestion is accepted, your Sim immediately goes to the phone and calls a cab. You have approximately half an hour before the cab arrives, which is just enough time to complete one Motive-directed activity. Go to the bathroom, brush your teeth, or do any other short-term activity that helps increase a Motive.

> **CAUTION**
> Remember, a Sim that you like doesn't necessarily feel the same way about you. Learn the relationship effects of each interaction, and keep a loose mental scorecard of your date candidate's daily Relationship score as you interact with him or her.

Usually, you should have no trouble getting a housemate to go with you, unless your Sims are having a spat. If so, simply talk a bit, or even offer an apology. This helps your Sims get back on the right track. Take a look at the interaction values and success criteria in chapter 10 to help you get your relationship built back up without too many failed interactions. After the date has been accepted, your Sim calls a cab, and both Sims get in when it arrives.

Fig. 14-3. As long as all is well at the homestead, you should always have an easy date with your housemates.

A good date can be a lifesaver for your household relationships. Time stands still in the home while your Sims are on their date, which means your Sims can get away for some quality one-on-one time without having to worry about what's going on at home. Going downtown is a perfect tool for bailing your Sims out of Motive slumps, too. Head downtown when your Sims need a break from a newborn baby or when you just can't seem to find time to squeeze in a meal. Instead of having these activities interrupted at home, you can indulge your Sims downtown. Plan your activities well, and you can return home with higher values in every Motive except for Energy.

Fig. 14-4. This Sim has just spent hours of time downtown but is no worse for wear other than a need for bed.

You may find that you can't quite put a face to a particular NPC name. Rather than take a gamble and find yourself downtown with the wrong Sim, pause the game and click on the Relationships tab. Scroll through the faces until you see the Sim you're looking for, and then click and hover to see that Sim's name and a summary of your relationship and their personality. Remember, their astrological sign gives you clues about their personality, so use the Zodiac information in chapter 1 to help you decide how to cater a date to his or her interests.

The Phone Call

If you don't live with the Sim you want to date, the phone is your best friend. You can reach any Sim in the neighborhood by phone, as long as they have a phone somewhere on their lot. You can also call any of the random NPCs that you've met downtown. These NPCs are listed under the last name, "Townie" in the phone call pie menu.

Fig. 14-5. Turn to the Relationships tab for a little pre-date research.

> **TIP** You may want to fill one lot with a "farm team" of eight Sims, and outfit their lot with nothing other than a table and a phone. Custom-design them to suit your single Sims, and then wait to run into them downtown or in the neighborhood!

After your invitation is accepted, your Sim hangs up and automatically calls a cab. Answer "Yes" when the dispatcher asks if you want to go downtown. You meet your date downtown, and you automatically greet each other as soon as you step out of the cab. After the automatic greeting, your date is officially underway!

The Pickup

You don't have to go downtown with a date in tow to find romance—the city is filled with NPCs just waiting for your Sim to ask them out! Of course, they may be waiting to tell your Sim "no," so you've still got to set up your proposition carefully. Either try a date with an NPC or neighborhood resident you've just met, or have an impromptu date with an established acquaintance that you happen to see downtown.

Fig. 14-6. As soon as you establish any kind of relationship with an NPC, he or she is saved along with your game so that you can see him or her again.

Either way, talk to your potential date before inviting him or her to spend some time with you. Ask about his or her interests, then talk about them. Remember, all interactions other than talking are now remembered by your Sims, and repeating the same one results in boredom and failure. Depending on your relationship, you may throw in a compliment, a friendly hug, or even a flirtation. When you're confident that your daily Relationship is high enough, select "Let's Date" to get the party started!

Choosing Your Venue

Now that you're officially on a date, it's time to decide where to go. The first decision is the downtown lot. If you picked up your date downtown, you're already on a lot, and it may be easiest to stay there. However, if you feel you'd have better luck elsewhere, you can go to any pay phone and call for a cab to take you and your date to a different lot.

Fig. 14-7. Don't feel trapped if you find yourself on an unfavorable lot with a date—just call a cab and go somewhere else.

As explained in chapter 12, your lots should cater to specific personality types, so you can maximize your dates with any given personality. Choose a lot that caters to the personality and Motive needs of your date. If you've just met your date, check out his or her personality with the Relationship display. If you still don't know where to go, choose a nice, generic lot that offers food, shopping, and fun group activities.

After you've settled on a lot, you still have to choose among the various activities available on the lot. Your cue for this decision is entirely based upon the magic question: "How are you?" Your date tells you (via a thought bubble) his or her lowest current Motive score. Usually, it will be hunger, because all NPCs downtown start the session with the same initial Motive scores as guests at your home, as listed in a table in chapter 7.

Fig. 14-8. Your two most important tools on a date are "How are you?" and "What are you into?"

Feed the need by heading to a restaurant. Click on the host podium and order the meal of your choice. The prices reflect the Hunger satisfaction value of the meal and affect how much your relationship improves when you suggest the meal to your date. As with most things downtown, money buys happiness, so if you can afford it, splurge.

Dining Out

A single successful meal can boost your daily Relationship score by more than 50 points. Much of this depends on the topic of conversation. If your Sims talk about something that strongly interests them both, they both get maximum Relationship score increases as they talk. Moderate interest levels in a topic result in lower gains to the relationship, and Sims who have little or no interest in the conversation see no change to their Relationship score.

Click on your Sim to change the topic of conversation. As mentioned in each of the invitation scenarios above, you've got to be familiar with your date's interests before you sit for the meal, steer the conversation toward those topics. If you can't remember or never checked, simply fish for conversation topics, and avoid those that result in a big red "X" through your date's thought bubble.

Fig. 14-9. Pay attention to the conversation, and change the topic if your date doesn't like what you're talking about.

If your Relationship score gets above 40, throw in an admiring glance for a big boost to both your daily and lifetime Relationship scores. Playing Footsie works if your date is both Playful and in a good mood, but if the meal is the first thing you've done, you might not have had enough time to boost their mood score from its starting value yet, which lowers your chance of success.

> **TIP** *Watch your date's reactions to your moves closely on a date, and pay special attention to a red drama mask. This response indicates that your date's overall mood is low, which means the failure was not necessarily an indication that his or her relationship with your Sim is too low.*

Don't try to Cuddle until your Sims are between courses. The Cuddle options are much more spicy than the standard table fare and require a stronger mood and relationship. After your date's tummy has been filled with a good meal and you've chatted your Social motives into the green, you have your best chance of scoring with an Embrace or a Kiss. Making Out requires a strong lifetime Relationship score, so don't even try it on a first date.

Fig. 14-10. Making Out may be immodest, but Sims with a close relationship have no shame when it comes to racking up daily Relationship points!

After dinner, head for the bathrooms. Your date's Bladder motive likely will be even lower than yours. It may take some time before everyone is done, but eventually you'll both make it through the crowds. Note the way the bathrooms draw crowds downtown, and use the experience to design functional bathroom areas when you're building them.

May I Buy You a Drink?

Bars provide you with some excellent opportunities on a date, whether it's your first date with a hottie or you're taking the ol' ball and chain for a spin around town. Tables near a bar are best on a date, because they spare your Sims some precious Energy while boosting their Comfort scores. Also, you can often get faster service at a table than you can in the crowds at the bar itself.

Fig. 14-11. Bar tables offer your Sims multiple Motive satisfactions, making them a better choice than stools or standing.

After you and your date are seated, click on the nearest Barmaid to order drinks. Your Sims stay seated, and the Barmaid comes over to take your order. You can talk with your date as you wait for your drinks. Eventually, the Barmaid returns with the drinks, and then the fun begins!

The drinks at the bar are so darn good, they put your Sims in a better mood. Each time a Sim takes a sip, his or her Relationship requirements for every interaction drop by one point. After a half dozen sips, a Kiss that used to require a Relationship score of 30 will be accepted with a just-got-to-know-you score of 24!

Fig. 14-12. May I buy you a drink? May I buy you five?

The promiscuity wears off after a little while, but the Relationship score changes do not. If you're having trouble breaking through to an ice queen (or king), thaw your date out with a few tasty beverages, and watch the soggy romance blossom. A session at the bar can be a turning point in a relationship between two Sims who don't share the same interests or personalities. The lowered Relationship score requirements open up some high-return interactions, allowing the couple to get "over the hump" so that their relationship can support those interactions without the aid of tasty libations.

Diamonds Are a Sim's Best Friend

Downtown is the perfect solution to all that extra cash your Sims have lying around. Retail shopping is a source of Fun, and it lets rich Sims buy their way into the hearts of those they adore. A gift requires very little for a successful reception, so you can give gifts before, during, or at the end of a date to pique your date's interest.

Shopping for Gifts

All gifts are not created equal. Each personality has a preferred type of gift, based upon interests. Romantic Sims are touched by flowers, even if they hardly know the giver. Playful Sims enjoy Lollipops, as well as a copy of *The Sims*. The following table describes each gift's required Relationship score for a successful interaction, as well as the personalities attracted to that gift. If a Sim is predisposed toward appreciating a certain gift, his or her relationship with your Sim can be much lower and he or she will still accept the gift. The table also lists the cost of each gift and the Relationship score effects of a successful gift. Note that a Sim who's in a terrible mood requires a stronger relationship to accept a gift.

Gifts

GIFT	COST	MINIMUM DAILY RELATIONSHIP	PERSONALITIES PLUS INTEREST ATTRACTED TO GIFT	DAILY CHANGE	LIFETIME CHANGE
Red Roses	200	10	Romance	+6	+3
Yellow Rose	50	10	Romance	+3	+1
Lollipop	25	0	Playful	+2	None
Chocolates	100	0	Food, Romance	+4	+2
Diamond Ring	1000	-40	Style, Money	+20	+10
Necklace	500	-30	Style, Money	+10	+5
The Zimz	150	0	Technology, Playful, Shy	+4	+1
Teddy Bear	200	0	Romance, 60's	+6	+3

Try giving your date a gift or two (in increasing value) at the beginning of the date to start out on the right foot. Your date's mood perks up a bit, setting up more successful interactions throughout the date. Always have a few gifts on hand on a date, so you can salvage a botched interaction. Gifts given at the end of a date are good for setting up your goodbye or an invitation home.

Fig. 14-13. Giving gifts is generally safe and easy, but choosing the right gift for your date is an art.

NOTE

You can also give gifts that you made yourself such as Preserves, Gnomes, and Paintings.

Frisky Business

You can also take your date shopping for clothes in the boutiques downtown. You can browse through the clothing racks, try new outfits on your Sim or your date, and even buy them. When you do, your new purchases show up in your armoire at home, available for your Sim to change into whenever he or she likes!

Fig. 14-14. Trying on clothes at the store leads to an elaborate sequence of evaluation and appreciation.

Your date can get very spicy in the clothing store. When your date tries on a new outfit, you have the undocumented option of clicking on the dressing booth and playing inside with your undressed date! Your date has to like you a *lot* for you to have any chance of success with this move, and a failed attempt is an instant date ender. If you're smooth, your Sims can frolic without a great deal of discretion, and come out much happier, if a bit unkempt.

All Good Things

Your date must eventually end, either because of fizzling interactions or low Motive levels. Better yet, if your date is really into you, you can invite him or her to come home with you! If you conduct the date well, you can end it on a positive note with a goodbye.

Fig. 14-15. A carefully crafted goodbye is the hallmark of a seasoned dater.

Your goodbye must match your relationship with your date. Intimate partners will be insulted by a simple Wave to mark the end of a date, while new friends will be shocked if you try to give them a romantic parting Kiss. Make your choice according to your Sim's relationship with your date. A botched goodbye leaves your date feeling angry or sad at the end of the evening, undoing some of the good work you did on the relationship.

Crash and Burn

A few circumstances bring a date to an immediate, flaming end. These exit conditions are to be avoided at all costs, unless you're actually looking to get crossed out of your date's little black book.

Date Enders
- **A rejected Kiss at the bar**
- **A rejected frolic in the dressing booth**
- **A failed Bladder (except as a result of an Extreme Tickle)**
- **Low Motives**

A Sim leaves a date if his or her Motive scores reach the same levels listed in chapter 7 on the Visitor Leaving table, with one exception. A Sim on a date will tolerate a Fun level of -90 before saying sayonara, which is much lower than the standard -55 that triggers house guests to leave. Even on a successful date, you can't stop Energy loss, so be sure you end your date before your date ends it for you!

Fig. 14-16. The date can get very hot in the dressing booth—or if rejected it might just end your date.

Fig. 14-17. You'll know when your date wanted to go home with you, but only after you've said goodbye. Remember the chance, and go for it next time.

Scoring Big

The ultimate end to a date is to get your date to come home with you for some shenanigans on the Love Seat or in the Love Tub. Your daily Relationship score should be very high before attempting this cheeky proposal, and your date should be in the mood for love. Don't leave it until the end of the outing, because you and your date will be too tired at that point. Plan a date from the start with the invitation home in mind, and save some Energy for your rendezvous back at your pad.

If you enjoy the visit enough, perhaps one time you might ask the Sim to move in, or even marry! When either happens, the Sim becomes a member of your household just like any other move-in or marriage. With the possibility of marriage to an NPC Sim, you can see your Sims through single life, dating, engagement, and even marriage, adding a whole new arc to the lives of your Sims.

CHAPTER 15:
EXTENDING YOUR WORLD

Introduction

Not that Maxis didn't pack *The Sims* with enough to do for months on end, but you can find additional tools, downloads, and links at the official website: *http://www.TheSims.com*. For the Sim hacker, the sky's the limit, thanks to an open game system that allows users to create and edit music and graphics files. The following sections give you a sneak peak at the free goodies awaiting you at the official *Sims* website.

Downloads

Art Studio!

Fig. 15-1. Click on the waving Sim for online help while using the program. Read the help windows, because the audio is in Sim-Speak.

This neat paint program lets you create original works of art for your Sims to buy, admire, and even sell. Your first step is to select a picture type (figure 15-2), which determines the size and style of painting.

Fig. 15-2. You can choose various sizes and designs for your picture, including a heart shape.

Next, you have the option to import any graphics file, regardless of size, as pictured in figure 15-3.

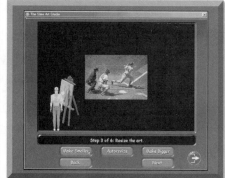

Fig. 15-3. We imported one of our favorite baseball pictures, then resized it to fit the painting window.

After selecting and sizing your picture, choose the texture and color of your frame, as pictured in figure 15-4.

Fig. 15-4. We opted for a rich walnut frame.

In the Catalog Info screen pictured here, set the price and enter a description of your new painting. Finally, save the painting. Choose a directory or use the default *UserObjects* subdirectory.

Fig. 15-5. After describing your painting and setting a price, save it to use in your game.

Sims File Cop

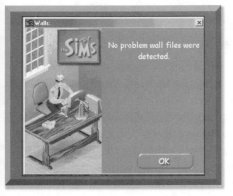

With all the files flying back and forth in the *Sims* community, you may inadvertently create or accept files that cause problems during a game session. The Sims File Cop examines your game directory for any damaged or risky files.

FaceLift

After playing *The Sims* for hours, you'll be ready for a few new faces in your neighborhood. After you register (no charge) at *The Sims* site, you can download FaceLift, a program that lets you create your own heads. You begin with a collection of nine randomly created heads, as pictured in figure 15-7. This is your starting point. If you don't see anything you like, click the Reset Faces button to create another set of nine.

Fig. 15-7. Begin by choosing a head.

Use a combination of the Blend and Deform buttons, along with the Mutation Rate slider bar, to create variations of the face. Change the head and hair together, or work separately on each area. The changes are not seen immediately, but when you go back to the main screen, you can review the altered face.

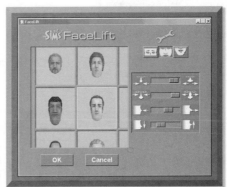

Fig. 15-8. The fine-tuning screen lets you change the size and shape of the nose, eyes, mouth, and jaw.

HomeCrafter

Fig. 15-9. HomeCrafter lets you view your creation in a Sims home setting.

This utility lets you design custom wallpapers and floors for your Sim houses. You create the patterns in any paint program, then use HomeCrafter to design the final product. If this sounds like too much work, check out one of the many *Sims* websites, such as *http://www.thesimsresource.com*, for thousands of user-created wallpapers (figure 15-10), floors (figure 15-11), and other items.

Fig. 15-10. Scroll through thousands of wallpaper designs and download your favorites.

Fig. 15-11. More than 2,300 floors and counting!

SimShow

Fig. 15-12. SimShow lets you check out your skins before importing them into the game.

If you've always wanted to create yourself or your favorite celebrity to use in *The Sims*, the SimShow utility is a must-have. After creating or editing a skin using any paint program, SimShow lets you view a Sim skin from various angles. You can alter the skin using your libraries of bodies, heads, body textures, and head textures, then apply various game animations to see your creation in action. The utility also comes with a skin library, and of course, you can supplement it from the thousands of skins available at *TheSims.com* or several other *Sims* websites.

Objects, Skins, and Homes

The official *Sims* website can get you started with a variety of files for your game. This site (*thesims.com*) has a page of links to other great Sims sites, such as *thesimsresource.com*.

...and a reflecting pool around the perimeter.

CAUTION

Remember to use File Cop to check the integrity of your Sims downloads.

NOTE

Most objects available on the website before House Party was released are included in House Party. Some are not included, however, like the new roses, the coming Potty Pack (porta-potties for The Sims), the trash pack, and the "Ukelele Lady Lamp."

Here are a few samples of what you can download from *TheSims.com*:

The Maximus house includes a workout room...

...spa room with multiple showers...

Your Sims can play with their new guinea pig and enjoy a bouquet of red roses.

It's murder on a budget, but you'll find it hard to pass up a pull on the new slot machine.

What Sim party animal wouldn't love a new jukebox?

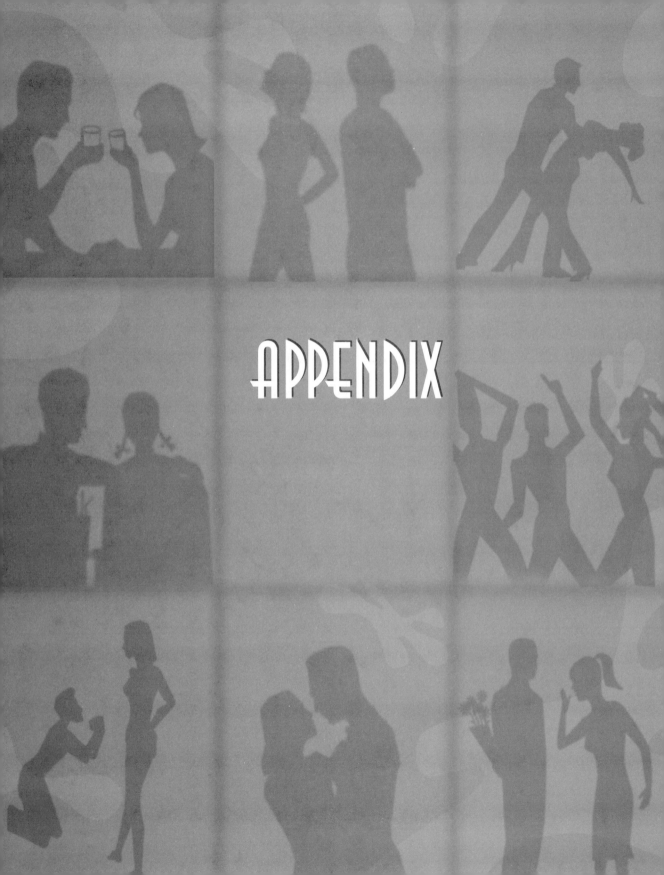

APPENDIX

Interaction Menu Triggers

CATEGORY	INTERACTION	RELATIONSHIP REQUIREMENTS	DISPOSITION REQUIREMENTS
Ask	How Are You?	Daily > -80	Mood > -70
Ask	How's Work?	Daily Between -5 and 35, Lifetime < 40	Mood > 0
Ask	Let's Hang Out/Date	None	Always Available Downtown
Ask	What Are You Into?	Daily Between -5 and 35, Lifetime < 40	Mood > 0
Attack	Fight	Daily < -40, Lifetime < 0	Mood < 0
Attack	Shove	Daily < -40, Lifetime <= 30	Mood < 0
Attack	Slap	Daily < -40, Lifetime <= 30	Mood < 0
Attack	Slapfight	Daily < -40	Playful >= 7, Mood < 0
Brag	Boast	None	Daily < 50, Lifetime < 40
Brag	Flex	Daily < 50, Lifetime < 40	Body >= 4
Brag	Primp	Daily < 50, Lifetime < 40	Charisma >= 2
Cheer Up	Comfort	Lifetime > 25, Friends	Outgoing > 3, Mood > 25, Subject's Mood < 0
	or	Lifetime > 5, Friends	Outgoing <= 3, Mood > 20, Subject's Mood < 0
Cheer Up	Encourage	Lifetime > 25, Friends	Charisma >= 2, Mood > 25
Cheer Up	With Puppet	Friends	Playful >= 6, Outgoing >= 4, Mood > 25, Subject's Mood < 0
Compliment	Admire	Daily Between -10 and 40	Mood > 20
Compliment	Worship	Daily Between -10 and 40, Lifetime Between 20 and 80	Nice > 3, Outgoing > 3, Mood > 20
Dance	Lively	Daily > 30, Lifetime > -25	Energy > 20, Mood > -20, Outgoing > 3
Dance	Slow	Lifetime > 20	Energy > 10
Entertain	Joke	Daily > 0, Lifetime Between -25 and 70	Playful >=3, Mood > -10
Entertain	Juggle	Daily > -25, Lifetime Between 0 and 70	Outgoing > 3, Playful > 4, Mood > 0
Entertain	With Puppet	Daily > -25, Lifetime Between 0 and 70	Outgoing > 3, Playful > 3, Mood > 0
Flirt	Check Out	Daily Between 5 and 60, Lifetime Between -10 and 10	Mood > -20
Flirt	Growl	Daily Between 5 and 60, Lifetime Between -10 and 10	Mood > -20

Interaction Menu Triggers, continued

CATEGORY	INTERACTION	RELATIONSHIP REQUIREMENTS	DISPOSITION REQUIREMENTS
Flirt	Backrub	Daily Between 30 and 60, Lifetime > 30	Mood > 30
Flirt	Sweet Talk	Daily Between 25 and 60, Lifetime > -50	Outgoing >= 7, Mood > 30
	or	Daily Between 40 and 60, Lifetime > -50	Outgoing < 7, Mood > 30
Greet	Wave	Always Available	
Greet	Shake Hands	Always Available	
Greet	Air Kiss	Lifetime >= 5	None
Greet	Kiss Cheek	Lifetime >= 20	None
Greet	Hug	Crush	None
Greet	Romantic Kiss	Crush	None
Greet	Suave Kiss	Lifetime > 15	Outgoing >= 3
Hug	Friendly	Lifetime > 0, Daily > 15	Mood > 10
Hug	Intimate	Lifetime > 10, Daily > 15	Mood > 20
Hug	Leap Into Arms	Daily > 40, Lifetime > 30	Mood > 25, Outgoing > 5
Hug	Romantic	Daily > 40, Lifetime > 40	Mood > 35, Outgoing > 3
Insult	Shake Fist	Lifetime < 50	Nice <= 3
	or	None	Mood < 0
Insult	Poke	Lifetime < 50	Nice <= 3
	or	None	Mood <= 0
Invite Downtown	None	None	At Home Only
Invite Home	None	Daily > 55	Downtown Only
Kiss	Peck	Daily >= 20, Lifetime > 0	Mood > 0
Kiss	Polite	Daily >= 35, Lifetime > 15	Mood > 15
Kiss	Suave	Daily >= 25, Lifetime > 10	Mood > 0
Kiss	Romantic	Daily >= 55, Lifetime > 25	Mood > 25
Kiss	Passionate	Daily >= 45, Lifetime > 25	Mood > 15
Kiss	Fiery Kiss	Love	Mood > 25
Nag	About Friends	Lifetime > 40	Mood <= -30
Nag	About House	Lifetime > 40	Mood <= -30
Nag	About Money	Lifetime > 40	Mood <= -30, Cash < §1,000
Plead	Apologize	Daily <= -10, Lifetime > 5	Mood <= -20
Plead	Grovel	Daily <= -20, Lifetime > 10	Mood <= -40
Proposition	Move In	Lifetime > 50, Daily > 50	Same Gender

Interaction Menu Triggers, continued

CATEGORY	INTERACTION	RELATIONSHIP REQUIREMENTS	DISPOSITION REQUIREMENTS
Proposition	Marriage	Daily > 75	Different Genders, In Love
Say Goodbye	Shoo	Daily < -50	None
Say Goodbye	Shake Hands	Daily > -50	None
Say Goodbye	Wave	Daily > -50	None
Say Goodbye	Kiss Cheek	Daily > -10	None
Say Goodbye	Hug	Daily > 0	None
Say Goodbye	Kiss Hand	Daily > 20	None
Say Goodbye	Polite Kiss	Daily >= 20	None
Say Goodbye	Passionate Kiss	Daily > 20	Outgoing >= 7
	or	Daily > 40	Outgoing < 7
Talk	About Interests	None	Available In Ongoing Conversation
Talk	Change Subject	None	Available In Ongoing Conversation
Talk	Gossip	None	Mood > -25
Tease	Imitate	None	Playful > 5, Mood < 15
	or	Daily < -20	Playful > 5, Nice < 5
Tease	Taunt	None	Mood < 30, Nice < 5
	or	Daily < -20	Nice < 5
Tease	Raspberry	None	Mood < 15, Nice < 5
	or	Daily < -20	Nice < 5
Tease	Scare	None	Playful >= 5, Mood < 30, Nice < 5
Tickle	Ribs	Daily > 10	Playful >= 4, Nice > 4
Tickle	Extreme	Daily > 10, Lifetime Between 20 and 70	Playful >= 4, Nice > 4

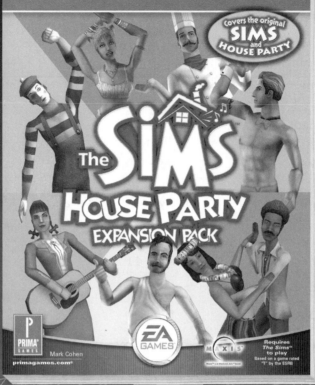

NOW AVAILABLE

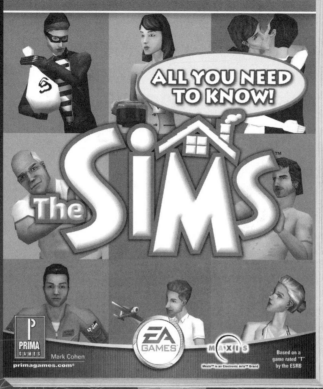

PRIMAGAMES.COM

Home
News
Strategy Guides
Forums
Game Worlds

www.primagames.com

More Than Just Strategy

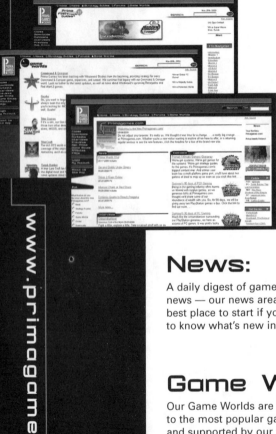

Strategy:

Over 250 Fast Track Guides with many more to come — new online strategy every week.

News:

A daily digest of game industry news — our news area is the best place to start if you want to know what's new in games.

Game Worlds:

Our Game Worlds are dedicated to the most popular games and supported by our wealth of Fan Site Affiliates.

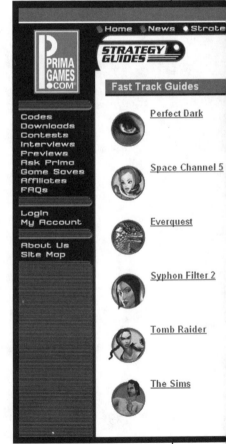

Strategy